ISBN: 1978474849
ISBN-13: 978-1978474840

Retro Kid

RETROKIDPUBLISHING.COM

DISTILLER: ....

AGE/EXPRESSION: ....

ORIGIN: .... **PRICE:** ....

SAMPLED: .... **RATING:** ☆ ☆ ☆ ☆ ☆

COLOR METER:

- MAHOGANY
- CARAMEL
- AMBER
- GOLD
- HONEY
- STRAW
- CLEAR

FLAVOR WHEEL:

HEAT/ABV: _____ %

BALANCE — FINISH — DARK FRUIT — CITRUS FRUIT — FLORAL — SPICY — HERBAL/GRASSY — MALT/CEREAL — TOFFEE — PEAT — SMOKE — SWEET — SALTY — ASTRINGENT — BODY

0.1 0.2 0.3 0.4 0.5

NOTES:

....

....

....

....

....

....

👉 **DISTILLER:** ....

AGE/EXPRESSION: ....

ORIGIN: .... **PRICE:** ....

SAMPLED: .... **RATING:** ☆ ☆ ☆ ☆ ☆

COLOR METER:

- MAHOGANY
- CARAMEL
- AMBER
- GOLD
- HONEY
- STRAW
- CLEAR

FLAVOR WHEEL:

HEAT/ _____ %
ABV: _____

FINISH
BALANCE
BODY
DARK FRUIT
ASTRIN-GENT
CITRUS FRUIT
SALTY
FLORAL
SWEET
SPICY
SMOKE
HERBAL/ GRASSY
PEAT
MALT/ CEREAL
TOFFEE

0.5 / 0.4 / 0.3 / 0.2 / 0.1

NOTES: ....

....

....

....

....

....

👉 **DISTILLER:** ....

AGE/EXPRESSION: ....

ORIGIN: .... **PRICE:** ....

SAMPLED: .... **RATING:** ☆ ☆ ☆ ☆ ☆

COLOR METER:

- MAHOGANY
- CARAMEL
- AMBER
- GOLD
- HONEY
- STRAW
- CLEAR

FLAVOR WHEEL:

HEAT/ABV : _____ %

BALANCE · FINISH · DARK FRUIT · CITRUS FRUIT · FLORAL · SPICY · HERBAL/GRASSY · MALT/CEREAL · TOFFEE · PEAT · SMOKE · SWEET · SALTY · ASTRINGENT · BODY

0.5 0.4 0.3 0.2 0.1

NOTES: ....

....

....

....

....

....

☞ DISTILLER: ....

AGE/EXPRESSION: ....

ORIGIN: .... PRICE: ....

SAMPLED: .... RATING: ☆ ☆ ☆ ☆ ☆

COLOR METER:

- MAHOGANY
- CARAMEL
- AMBER
- GOLD
- HONEY
- STRAW
- CLEAR

FLAVOR WHEEL:

HEAT/ _____ %
ABV: _____

BALANCE
FINISH
BODY
DARK FRUIT
ASTRIN-GENT
CITRUS FRUIT
SALTY
FLORAL
SWEET
SPICY
SMOKE
HERBAL/ GRASSY
PEAT
TOFFEE
MALT/ CEREAL

05
04
03
02
01

NOTES:

....

....

....

....

....

....

DISTILLER: ....

AGE/EXPRESSION: ....

ORIGIN: .... PRICE: ....

SAMPLED: .... RATING: ☆ ☆ ☆ ☆ ☆

COLOR METER:

- MAHOGANY
- CARAMEL
- AMBER
- GOLD
- HONEY
- STRAW
- CLEAR

FLAVOR WHEEL:

HEAT/ABV: _____ %

BALANCE · FINISH · DARK FRUIT · CITRUS FRUIT · FLORAL · SPICY · HERBAL/GRASSY · MALT/CEREAL · TOFFEE · PEAT · SMOKE · SWEET · SALTY · ASTRINGENT · BODY

0.1 0.2 0.3 0.4 0.5

NOTES:

....
....
....
....
....
....

👉 **DISTILLER:** ....

AGE/EXPRESSION: ....

ORIGIN: .... **PRICE:** ....

SAMPLED: .... **RATING:** ☆ ☆ ☆ ☆ ☆

COLOR METER:

- MAHOGANY
- CARAMEL
- AMBER
- GOLD
- HONEY
- STRAW
- CLEAR

FLAVOR WHEEL:

HEAT/ABV: _____ %

BALANCE · FINISH · DARK FRUIT · CITRUS FRUIT · FLORAL · SPICY · HERBAL/GRASSY · MALT/CEREAL · TOFFEE · PEAT · SMOKE · SWEET · SALTY · ASTRINGENT · BODY

0.1 0.2 0.3 0.4 0.5

NOTES:

....
....
....
....
....
....

DISTILLER: ....

AGE/EXPRESSION: ....

ORIGIN: .... **PRICE:** ....

SAMPLED: .... **RATING:** ☆☆☆☆☆

COLOR METER:

- MAHOGANY
- CARAMEL
- AMBER
- GOLD
- HONEY
- STRAW
- CLEAR

FLAVOR WHEEL:

HEAT/ABV: _____ %

BALANCE
FINISH
BODY
DARK FRUIT
ASTRIN-GENT
CITRUS FRUIT
SALTY
FLORAL
SWEET
SPICY
SMOKE
HERBAL/GRASSY
PEAT
TOFFEE
MALT/CEREAL

0.1 0.2 0.3 0.4 0.5

NOTES:

....
....
....
....
....

DISTILLER: ....

AGE/EXPRESSION: ....

ORIGIN: ....   PRICE: ....

SAMPLED: ....   RATING: ☆☆☆☆☆

COLOR METER:

- MAHOGANY
- CARAMEL
- AMBER
- GOLD
- HONEY
- STRAW
- CLEAR

FLAVOR WHEEL:

HEAT/ABV: _____ %

BALANCE
FINISH
BODY
DARK FRUIT
ASTRIN-GENT
CITRUS FRUIT
SALTY
FLORAL
SWEET
SPICY
SMOKE
HERBAL/GRASSY
PEAT
MALT/CEREAL
TOFFEE

0.1 0.2 0.3 0.4 0.5

NOTES:

....
....
....
....
....
....

DISTILLER: ....

AGE/EXPRESSION: ....

ORIGIN: ....   **PRICE:** ....

SAMPLED: ....   **RATING:** ☆ ☆ ☆ ☆ ☆

COLOR METER:

- MAHOGANY
- CARAMEL
- AMBER
- GOLD
- HONEY
- STRAW
- CLEAR

FLAVOR WHEEL:

HEAT/ABV: _____ %

BALANCE · FINISH · BODY · DARK FRUIT · ASTRINGENT · CITRUS FRUIT · SALTY · FLORAL · SWEET · SPICY · SMOKE · HERBAL/GRASSY · PEAT · TOFFEE · MALT/CEREAL

0.1 0.2 0.3 0.4 0.5

NOTES:

....
....
....
....
....
....

👉 **DISTILLER:** . . . .

AGE/EXPRESSION: . . . .

ORIGIN: . . . . **PRICE:** . . . .

SAMPLED: . . . . **RATING:** ☆ ☆ ☆ ☆ ☆

COLOR METER:

- MAHOGANY
- CARAMEL
- AMBER
- GOLD
- HONEY
- STRAW
- CLEAR

FLAVOR WHEEL:

HEAT/ABV: _____ %

BALANCE · FINISH · DARK FRUIT · CITRUS FRUIT · FLORAL · SPICY · HERBAL/GRASSY · MALT/CEREAL · TOFFEE · PEAT · SMOKE · SWEET · SALTY · ASTRINGENT · BODY

0.5 0.4 0.3 0.2 0.1

NOTES: . . . .
. . . .
. . . .
. . . .
. . . .
. . . .

DISTILLER: ....

AGE/EXPRESSION: ....

ORIGIN: .... PRICE: ....

SAMPLED: .... RATING: ☆☆☆☆☆

COLOR METER:

- MAHOGANY
- CARAMEL
- AMBER
- GOLD
- HONEY
- STRAW
- CLEAR

FLAVOR WHEEL:

HEAT/ABV: .... %

BALANCE
FINISH
BODY
DARK FRUIT
ASTRIN-GENT
CITRUS FRUIT
SALTY
FLORAL
SWEET
SPICY
SMOKE
HERBAL/GRASSY
PEAT
TOFFEE
MALT/CEREAL

0.1 0.2 0.3 0.4 0.5

NOTES:

....
....
....
....
....

DISTILLER: ....

AGE/EXPRESSION: ....

ORIGIN: .... PRICE: ....

SAMPLED: .... RATING: ☆ ☆ ☆ ☆ ☆

COLOR METER:

- MAHOGANY
- CARAMEL
- AMBER
- GOLD
- HONEY
- STRAW
- CLEAR

FLAVOR WHEEL:

HEAT/ _____ %
ABV: _____

BALANCE   FINISH

BODY   DARK FRUIT

ASTRIN-GENT   CITRUS FRUIT

SALTY   FLORAL

SWEET   SPICY

SMOKE   HERBAL/GRASSY

PEAT   TOFFEE   MALT/CEREAL

0.5
0.4
0.3
0.2
0.1

NOTES:

....
....
....
....
....
....

DISTILLER: . . . .

AGE/EXPRESSION: . . . .

ORIGIN: . . . . PRICE: . . . .

SAMPLED: . . . . RATING: ☆ ☆ ☆ ☆ ☆

COLOR METER:

- MAHOGANY
- CARAMEL
- AMBER
- GOLD
- HONEY
- STRAW
- CLEAR

FLAVOR WHEEL:

HEAT/ABV: . . . . %

FINISH
BALANCE
BODY
DARK FRUIT
ASTRIN-GENT
CITRUS FRUIT
SALTY
FLORAL
SWEET
SPICY
SMOKE
HERBAL/GRASSY
PEAT
MALT/CEREAL
TOFFEE

0.1 0.2 0.3 0.4 0.5

NOTES:

. . . .

. . . .

. . . .

. . . .

. . . .

. . . .

DISTILLER: . . . .

AGE/EXPRESSION: . . . .

ORIGIN: . . . . PRICE: . . . .

SAMPLED: . . . . RATING: ☆ ☆ ☆ ☆ ☆

COLOR METER:

- MAHOGANY
- CARAMEL
- AMBER
- GOLD
- HONEY
- STRAW
- CLEAR

FLAVOR WHEEL:

HEAT/ABV: _____ %

BALANCE
FINISH
BODY
DARK FRUIT
ASTRIN-GENT
CITRUS FRUIT
SALTY
FLORAL
SWEET
SPICY
SMOKE
HERBAL/GRASSY
PEAT
TOFFEE
MALT/CEREAL

0.1 0.2 0.3 0.4 0.5

NOTES:

. . . .

. . . .

. . . .

. . . .

. . . .

DISTILLER: ....

AGE/EXPRESSION: ....

ORIGIN: .... PRICE: ....

SAMPLED: .... RATING: ☆ ☆ ☆ ☆ ☆

COLOR METER:

- MAHOGANY
- CARAMEL
- AMBER
- GOLD
- HONEY
- STRAW
- CLEAR

FLAVOR WHEEL:

HEAT/ABV: _____ %

BALANCE — FINISH

BODY — DARK FRUIT

ASTRIN-GENT — CITRUS FRUIT

SALTY — FLORAL

SWEET — SPICY

SMOKE — HERBAL/GRASSY

PEAT — TOFFEE — MALT/CEREAL

0.1 0.2 0.3 0.4 0.5

NOTES:

....
....
....
....
....

DISTILLER: ....

AGE/EXPRESSION: ....

ORIGIN: .... PRICE: ....

SAMPLED: .... RATING: ☆ ☆ ☆ ☆ ☆

COLOR METER:

- MAHOGANY
- CARAMEL
- AMBER
- GOLD
- HONEY
- STRAW
- CLEAR

FLAVOR WHEEL:

HEAT/ABV: _____ %

BALANCE
FINISH
BODY
DARK FRUIT
ASTRIN-GENT
CITRUS FRUIT
SALTY
FLORAL
SWEET
SPICY
SMOKE
HERBAL/GRASSY
PEAT
MALT/CEREAL
TOFFEE

0.1 0.2 0.3 0.4 0.5

NOTES:

....
....
....
....
....
....

👉 **DISTILLER:** ....

AGE/EXPRESSION: ....

ORIGIN: .... **PRICE:** ....

SAMPLED: .... **RATING:** ☆☆☆☆☆

COLOR METER:

- MAHOGANY
- CARAMEL
- AMBER
- GOLD
- HONEY
- STRAW
- CLEAR

FLAVOR WHEEL:

HEAT/ABV: _____ %

BALANCE · FINISH · DARK FRUIT · CITRUS FRUIT · FLORAL · SPICY · HERBAL/GRASSY · MALT/CEREAL · TOFFEE · PEAT · SMOKE · SWEET · SALTY · ASTRINGENT · BODY

0.1 0.2 0.3 0.4 0.5

NOTES:

....
....
....
....
....

👉 DISTILLER: ....

AGE/EXPRESSION: ....

ORIGIN: .... PRICE: ....

SAMPLED: .... RATING: ☆☆☆☆☆

COLOR METER:

- MAHOGANY
- CARAMEL
- AMBER
- GOLD
- HONEY
- STRAW
- CLEAR

FLAVOR WHEEL:

HEAT/ABV: _____ %

FINISH
BALANCE
BODY
DARK FRUIT
ASTRIN-GENT
CITRUS FRUIT
SALTY
FLORAL
SWEET
SPICY
SMOKE
HERBAL/GRASSY
PEAT
MALT/CEREAL
TOFFEE

05
04
03
02
01

NOTES:

....
....
....
....
....
....

DISTILLER: ....

AGE/EXPRESSION: ....

ORIGIN: .... PRICE: ....

SAMPLED: .... RATING: ☆ ☆ ☆ ☆ ☆

COLOR METER:

- MAHOGANY
- CARAMEL
- AMBER
- GOLD
- HONEY
- STRAW
- CLEAR

FLAVOR WHEEL:

HEAT/ABV: .... %

BALANCE
FINISH
BODY
DARK FRUIT
ASTRIN-GENT
CITRUS FRUIT
SALTY
FLORAL
SWEET
SPICY
SMOKE
HERBAL/GRASSY
PEAT
TOFFEE
MALT/CEREAL

0.5
0.4
0.3
0.2
0.1

NOTES:

....

....

....

....

....

👉 **DISTILLER:** ....

AGE/EXPRESSION: ....

ORIGIN: .... **PRICE:** ....

SAMPLED: .... **RATING:** ☆☆☆☆☆

COLOR METER:

- MAHOGANY
- CARAMEL
- AMBER
- GOLD
- HONEY
- STRAW
- CLEAR

FLAVOR WHEEL:

HEAT/ABV: _____ %

BALANCE · FINISH · DARK FRUIT · CITRUS FRUIT · FLORAL · SPICY · HERBAL/GRASSY · MALT/CEREAL · TOFFEE · PEAT · SMOKE · SWEET · SALTY · ASTRINGENT · BODY

0.1 0.2 0.3 0.4 0.5

NOTES:

....
....
....
....
....
....

👉 DISTILLER: ....

AGE/EXPRESSION: ....

ORIGIN: ....   PRICE: ....

SAMPLED: ....   RATING: ☆ ☆ ☆ ☆ ☆

COLOR METER:

- MAHOGANY
- CARAMEL
- AMBER
- GOLD
- HONEY
- STRAW
- CLEAR

FLAVOR WHEEL:

HEAT/ABV: _____ %

BALANCE · FINISH · DARK FRUIT · CITRUS FRUIT · FLORAL · SPICY · HERBAL/GRASSY · MALT/CEREAL · TOFFEE · PEAT · SMOKE · SWEET · SALTY · ASTRINGENT · BODY

0.5 0.4 0.3 0.2 0.1

NOTES:

....

....

....

....

....

DISTILLER: ....

AGE/EXPRESSION: ....

ORIGIN: .... PRICE: ....

SAMPLED: .... RATING: ☆ ☆ ☆ ☆ ☆

COLOR METER:

- MAHOGANY
- CARAMEL
- AMBER
- GOLD
- HONEY
- STRAW
- CLEAR

FLAVOR WHEEL:

HEAT / ABV: _____ %

BALANCE
FINISH
BODY
DARK FRUIT
ASTRIN-GENT
CITRUS FRUIT
SALTY
FLORAL
SWEET
SPICY
SMOKE
HERBAL/GRASSY
PEAT
TOFFEE
MALT/CEREAL

0.5
0.4
0.3
0.2
0.1

NOTES:

....
....
....
....
....
....

👉 DISTILLER: ....

AGE/EXPRESSION: ....

ORIGIN: .... PRICE: ....

SAMPLED: .... RATING: ☆ ☆ ☆ ☆ ☆

COLOR METER:

- MAHOGANY
- CARAMEL
- AMBER
- GOLD
- HONEY
- STRAW
- CLEAR

FLAVOR WHEEL:

HEAT/ABV: _____ %

BALANCE
FINISH
BODY
DARK FRUIT
ASTRIN-GENT
CITRUS FRUIT
SALTY
FLORAL
SWEET
SPICY
SMOKE
HERBAL/GRASSY
PEAT
MALT/CEREAL
TOFFEE

0.1 0.2 0.3 0.4 0.5

NOTES:

....
....
....
....
....
....

☞ **DISTILLER:** ....

AGE/EXPRESSION: ....

ORIGIN: .... **PRICE:** ....

SAMPLED: .... **RATING:** ☆☆☆☆☆

COLOR METER:

- MAHOGANY
- CARAMEL
- AMBER
- GOLD
- HONEY
- STRAW
- CLEAR

FLAVOR WHEEL:

HEAT/ABV: _____ %

BALANCE
FINISH
BODY
DARK FRUIT
ASTRIN-GENT
CITRUS FRUIT
SALTY
FLORAL
SWEET
SPICY
SMOKE
HERBAL/GRASSY
PEAT
TOFFEE
MALT/CEREAL

0.5
0.4
0.3
0.2
0.1

NOTES:

....

....

....

....

....

....

DISTILLER: ....

AGE/EXPRESSION: ....

ORIGIN: .... **PRICE:** ....

SAMPLED: .... **RATING:** ☆ ☆ ☆ ☆ ☆

COLOR METER:

- MAHOGANY
- CARAMEL
- AMBER
- GOLD
- HONEY
- STRAW
- CLEAR

FLAVOR WHEEL:

HEAT/ABV: _____ %

BALANCE
FINISH
BODY
DARK FRUIT
ASTRIN-GENT
CITRUS FRUIT
SALTY
FLORAL
SWEET
SPICY
SMOKE
HERBAL/GRASSY
PEAT
MALT/CEREAL
TOFFEE

0.5 0.4 0.3 0.2 0.1

NOTES:

....

....

....

....

....

....

👉 **DISTILLER:** . . . .

AGE/EXPRESSION: . . . .

ORIGIN: . . . . **PRICE:** . . . .

SAMPLED: . . . . **RATING:** ☆ ☆ ☆ ☆ ☆

COLOR METER:

- MAHOGANY
- CARAMEL
- AMBER
- GOLD
- HONEY
- STRAW
- CLEAR

FLAVOR WHEEL:

HEAT / . . . . . . %
ABV: . . . .

BALANCE
FINISH
BODY
DARK FRUIT
ASTRIN-GENT
CITRUS FRUIT
SALTY
FLORAL
SWEET
SPICY
SMOKE
HERBAL/ GRASSY
PEAT
TOFFEE
MALT/ CEREAL

0.5 0.4 0.3 0.2 0.1

NOTES:

. . . .

. . . .

. . . .

. . . .

. . . .

👉 DISTILLER: ....

AGE/EXPRESSION: ....

ORIGIN: .... PRICE: ....

SAMPLED: .... RATING: ☆☆☆☆☆

COLOR METER:

- MAHOGANY
- CARAMEL
- AMBER
- GOLD
- HONEY
- STRAW
- CLEAR

FLAVOR WHEEL:

HEAT/ _____ %
ABV: _____

BALANCE FINISH DARK FRUIT

BODY CITRUS FRUIT

ASTRIN-GENT FLORAL

SALTY SPICY

SWEET HERBAL/GRASSY

SMOKE MALT/CEREAL

PEAT TOFFEE

0.1 0.2 0.3 0.4 0.5

NOTES:

....

....

....

....

....

👉 **DISTILLER:** ....

AGE/EXPRESSION: ....

ORIGIN: .... **PRICE:** ....

SAMPLED: .... **RATING:** ☆☆☆☆☆

COLOR METER:

- MAHOGANY
- CARAMEL
- AMBER
- GOLD
- HONEY
- STRAW
- CLEAR

FLAVOR WHEEL:

HEAT/ _____ %
ABV: _____

BALANCE
FINISH
BODY
DARK FRUIT
ASTRIN-GENT
CITRUS FRUIT
SALTY
FLORAL
SWEET
SPICY
SMOKE
HERBAL/ GRASSY
PEAT
TOFFEE
MALT/ CEREAL

0.5
0.4
0.3
0.2
0.1

NOTES: ....
....
....
....
....
....

DISTILLER: . . . .

AGE/EXPRESSION: . . . .

ORIGIN: . . . . PRICE: . . . .

SAMPLED: . . . . RATING: ☆ ☆ ☆ ☆ ☆

COLOR METER:

- MAHOGANY
- CARAMEL
- AMBER
- GOLD
- HONEY
- STRAW
- CLEAR

FLAVOR WHEEL:

HEAT/ABV: . . . . %

BALANCE   FINISH
BODY   DARK FRUIT
ASTRIN-GENT   CITRUS FRUIT
SALTY   FLORAL
SWEET   SPICY
SMOKE   HERBAL/GRASSY
PEAT   TOFFEE   MALT/CEREAL

0.5
0.4
0.3
0.2
0.1

NOTES:
. . . .
. . . .
. . . .
. . . .
. . . .

👉 **DISTILLER:** . . . .

AGE/EXPRESSION: . . . .

ORIGIN: . . . . **PRICE:** . . . .

SAMPLED: . . . . **RATING:** ☆ ☆ ☆ ☆ ☆

COLOR METER:

- MAHOGANY
- CARAMEL
- AMBER
- GOLD
- HONEY
- STRAW
- CLEAR

FLAVOR WHEEL:

HEAT / ABV: _____ %

BALANCE, FINISH, DARK FRUIT, CITRUS FRUIT, FLORAL, SPICY, HERBAL / GRASSY, MALT / CEREAL, TOFFEE, PEAT, SMOKE, SWEET, SALTY, ASTRIN-GENT, BODY

0.1 0.2 0.3 0.4 0.5

NOTES: . . . .

. . . .

. . . .

. . . .

. . . .

. . . .

DISTILLER: ....

AGE/EXPRESSION: ....

ORIGIN: .... PRICE: ....

SAMPLED: .... RATING: ☆☆☆☆☆

COLOR METER:

- MAHOGANY
- CARAMEL
- AMBER
- GOLD
- HONEY
- STRAW
- CLEAR

FLAVOR WHEEL:

HEAT/ABV: _____ %

BALANCE
FINISH
BODY
DARK FRUIT
ASTRIN-GENT
CITRUS FRUIT
SALTY
FLORAL
SWEET
SPICY
SMOKE
HERBAL/GRASSY
PEAT
MALT/CEREAL
TOFFEE

0.1 0.2 0.3 0.4 0.5

NOTES:

....
....
....
....
....

👉 **DISTILLER:** ....

AGE/EXPRESSION: ....

ORIGIN: .... **PRICE:** ....

SAMPLED: .... **RATING:** ☆ ☆ ☆ ☆ ☆

COLOR METER:

- MAHOGANY
- CARAMEL
- AMBER
- GOLD
- HONEY
- STRAW
- CLEAR

FLAVOR WHEEL:

HEAT/ ABV: _____ %

BALANCE · FINISH · DARK FRUIT · CITRUS FRUIT · FLORAL · SPICY · HERBAL/GRASSY · MALT/CEREAL · TOFFEE · PEAT · SMOKE · SWEET · SALTY · ASTRINGENT · BODY

0.1 0.2 0.3 0.4 0.5

NOTES: ....
....
....
....
....
....

☞ **DISTILLER:** ....

AGE/EXPRESSION: ....

ORIGIN: .... **PRICE:** ....

SAMPLED: .... **RATING:** ☆☆☆☆☆

COLOR METER:

- MAHOGANY
- CARAMEL
- AMBER
- GOLD
- HONEY
- STRAW
- CLEAR

FLAVOR WHEEL:

HEAT/
ABV: _____ %

BALANCE
FINISH
BODY
DARK FRUIT
ASTRIN-GENT
CITRUS FRUIT
SALTY
FLORAL
SWEET
SPICY
SMOKE
HERBAL/GRASSY
PEAT
TOFFEE
MALT/CEREAL

0.5
0.4
0.3
0.2
0.1

NOTES:

....
....
....
....
....
....

☞ **DISTILLER:** ....

AGE/EXPRESSION: ....

ORIGIN: .... **PRICE:** ....

SAMPLED: .... **RATING:** ☆ ☆ ☆ ☆ ☆

COLOR METER:

- MAHOGANY
- CARAMEL
- AMBER
- GOLD
- HONEY
- STRAW
- CLEAR

FLAVOR WHEEL:

HEAT/ABV: _____ %

BALANCE · FINISH · DARK FRUIT · CITRUS FRUIT · FLORAL · SPICY · HERBAL/GRASSY · MALT/CEREAL · TOFFEE · PEAT · SMOKE · SWEET · SALTY · ASTRINGENT · BODY

0.5 0.4 0.3 0.2 0.1

NOTES: ....
....
....
....
....
....

👉 DISTILLER: ....

AGE/EXPRESSION: ....

ORIGIN: .... PRICE: ....

SAMPLED: .... RATING: ☆ ☆ ☆ ☆ ☆

COLOR METER:

- MAHOGANY
- CARAMEL
- AMBER
- GOLD
- HONEY
- STRAW
- CLEAR

FLAVOR WHEEL:

HEAT/ABV: _____ %

BALANCE
FINISH
BODY
DARK FRUIT
ASTRIN-GENT
CITRUS FRUIT
SALTY
FLORAL
SWEET
SPICY
SMOKE
HERBAL/GRASSY
PEAT
MALT/CEREAL
TOFFEE

0.5 0.4 0.3 0.2 0.1

NOTES:
....
....
....
....
....
....

👉 **DISTILLER:** ....

AGE/EXPRESSION: ....

ORIGIN: .... **PRICE:** ....

SAMPLED: .... **RATING:** ☆☆☆☆☆

COLOR METER:

- MAHOGANY
- CARAMEL
- AMBER
- GOLD
- HONEY
- STRAW
- CLEAR

FLAVOR WHEEL:

HEAT/ABV: _____ %

FINISH

BALANCE

BODY

DARK FRUIT

ASTRIN-GENT

CITRUS FRUIT

SALTY

FLORAL

SWEET

SPICY

SMOKE

HERBAL/GRASSY

PEAT

MALT/CEREAL

TOFFEE

(axis values: 01, 02, 03, 04, 05)

NOTES:

....
....
....
....
....
....

👉 DISTILLER: ....

AGE/EXPRESSION: ....

ORIGIN: .... PRICE: ....

SAMPLED: .... RATING: ☆☆☆☆☆

COLOR METER:

- MAHOGANY
- CARAMEL
- AMBER
- GOLD
- HONEY
- STRAW
- CLEAR

FLAVOR WHEEL:

HEAT/
ABV: _____ %

BALANCE
FINISH
BODY
DARK FRUIT
ASTRIN-GENT
CITRUS FRUIT
SALTY
FLORAL
SWEET
SPICY
SMOKE
HERBAL/GRASSY
PEAT
TOFFEE
MALT/CEREAL

0.5
0.4
0.3
0.2
0.1

NOTES:

....

....

....

....

....

☞ **DISTILLER:** ....

AGE/EXPRESSION: ....

ORIGIN: .... **PRICE:** ....

SAMPLED: .... **RATING:** ☆☆☆☆☆

COLOR METER:

- MAHOGANY
- CARAMEL
- AMBER
- GOLD
- HONEY
- STRAW
- CLEAR

FLAVOR WHEEL:

HEAT/ABV: _____ %

BALANCE — FINISH — DARK FRUIT — CITRUS FRUIT — FLORAL — SPICY — HERBAL/GRASSY — MALT/CEREAL — TOFFEE — PEAT — SMOKE — SWEET — SALTY — ASTRINGENT — BODY

05 04 03 02 01

NOTES: ....
....
....
....
....
....

☞ DISTILLER: ....

AGE/EXPRESSION: ....
....

ORIGIN: .... PRICE: ....

SAMPLED: .... RATING: ☆☆☆☆☆

COLOR METER:

- MAHOGANY
- CARAMEL
- AMBER
- GOLD
- HONEY
- STRAW
- CLEAR

FLAVOR WHEEL:

HEAT/ABV: _____ %

BALANCE · FINISH · DARK FRUIT · CITRUS FRUIT · FLORAL · SPICY · HERBAL/GRASSY · MALT/CEREAL · TOFFEE · PEAT · SMOKE · SWEET · SALTY · ASTRINGENT · BODY

0.1 0.2 0.3 0.4 0.5

NOTES:

....
....
....
....
....
....

DISTILLER: ....

AGE/EXPRESSION: ....

ORIGIN: .... **PRICE:** ....

SAMPLED: .... **RATING:** ☆ ☆ ☆ ☆ ☆

COLOR METER:

- MAHOGANY
- CARAMEL
- AMBER
- GOLD
- HONEY
- STRAW
- CLEAR

FLAVOR WHEEL:

HEAT / ABV: _____ %

BALANCE, FINISH, BODY, DARK FRUIT, ASTRIN-GENT, CITRUS FRUIT, SALTY, FLORAL, SWEET, SPICY, SMOKE, HERBAL/GRASSY, PEAT, TOFFEE, MALT/CEREAL

0.1 0.2 0.3 0.4 0.5

NOTES:

....
....
....
....
....
....

DISTILLER: ....

AGE/EXPRESSION: ....

ORIGIN: .... **PRICE:** ....

SAMPLED: .... **RATING:** ☆ ☆ ☆ ☆ ☆

COLOR METER:

- MAHOGANY
- CARAMEL
- AMBER
- GOLD
- HONEY
- STRAW
- CLEAR

FLAVOR WHEEL:

HEAT/ABV: _____ %

FINISH
BALANCE
BODY
DARK FRUIT
ASTRIN-GENT
CITRUS FRUIT
SALTY
FLORAL
SWEET
SPICY
SMOKE
HERBAL/GRASSY
PEAT
TOFFEE
MALT/CEREAL

0.5
0.4
0.3
0.2
0.1

NOTES:
....
....
....
....
....

DISTILLER: ....

AGE/EXPRESSION: ....

ORIGIN: .... PRICE: ....

SAMPLED: .... RATING: ☆ ☆ ☆ ☆ ☆

COLOR METER:

- MAHOGANY
- CARAMEL
- AMBER
- GOLD
- HONEY
- STRAW
- CLEAR

FLAVOR WHEEL:

HEAT/ _____ %
ABV: _____

BALANCE
FINISH
BODY
DARK FRUIT
ASTRIN-GENT
CITRUS FRUIT
SALTY
FLORAL
SWEET
SPICY
SMOKE
HERBAL/GRASSY
PEAT
MALT/CEREAL
TOFFEE

0.5
0.4
0.3
0.2
0.1

NOTES:

....
....
....
....
....
....

👉 **DISTILLER:** ....

AGE/EXPRESSION: ....

ORIGIN: .... **PRICE:** ....

SAMPLED: .... **RATING:** ☆☆☆☆☆

COLOR METER:

- MAHOGANY
- CARAMEL
- AMBER
- GOLD
- HONEY
- STRAW
- CLEAR

FLAVOR WHEEL:

HEAT/ABV: _____ %

BALANCE
FINISH
BODY
DARK FRUIT
ASTRIN-GENT
CITRUS FRUIT
SALTY
FLORAL
SWEET
SPICY
SMOKE
HERBAL/GRASSY
PEAT
TOFFEE
MALT/CEREAL

0.1 0.2 0.3 0.4 0.5

NOTES:

....
....
....
....
....
....

DISTILLER: ....

AGE/EXPRESSION: ....

ORIGIN: .... **PRICE:** ....

SAMPLED: .... **RATING:** ☆☆☆☆☆

COLOR METER:

- MAHOGANY
- CARAMEL
- AMBER
- GOLD
- HONEY
- STRAW
- CLEAR

FLAVOR WHEEL:

HEAT/ ____ %
ABV: ____

BALANCE
FINISH
BODY
DARK FRUIT
ASTRIN-GENT
CITRUS FRUIT
SALTY
FLORAL
SWEET
SPICY
SMOKE
HERBAL/ GRASSY
PEAT
MALT/ CEREAL
TOFFEE

0.5
0.4
0.3
0.2
0.1

NOTES:
....
....
....
....
....
....

DISTILLER: ....

AGE/EXPRESSION: ....

ORIGIN: .... **PRICE:** ....

SAMPLED: .... **RATING:** ☆ ☆ ☆ ☆ ☆

COLOR METER:

- MAHOGANY
- CARAMEL
- AMBER
- GOLD
- HONEY
- STRAW
- CLEAR

FLAVOR WHEEL:

HEAT/ABV: _____ %

BALANCE · FINISH · DARK FRUIT · CITRUS FRUIT · FLORAL · SPICY · HERBAL/GRASSY · MALT/CEREAL · TOFFEE · PEAT · SMOKE · SWEET · SALTY · ASTRINGENT · BODY

0.1 · 0.2 · 0.3 · 0.4 · 0.5

NOTES:
....
....
....
....
....

DISTILLER: ....

AGE/EXPRESSION: ....

ORIGIN: .... **PRICE:** ....

SAMPLED: .... **RATING:** ☆ ☆ ☆ ☆ ☆

COLOR METER:

- MAHOGANY
- CARAMEL
- AMBER
- GOLD
- HONEY
- STRAW
- CLEAR

FLAVOR WHEEL:

HEAT / ABV: _____ %

BALANCE · FINISH · DARK FRUIT · CITRUS FRUIT · FLORAL · SPICY · HERBAL/GRASSY · MALT/CEREAL · TOFFEE · PEAT · SMOKE · SWEET · SALTY · ASTRINGENT · BODY

05 04 03 02 01

NOTES:

....

....

....

....

....

DISTILLER: ....

AGE/EXPRESSION: ....

ORIGIN: .... **PRICE:** ....

SAMPLED: .... **RATING:** ☆ ☆ ☆ ☆ ☆

COLOR METER:

- MAHOGANY
- CARAMEL
- AMBER
- GOLD
- HONEY
- STRAW
- CLEAR

FLAVOR WHEEL:

HEAT/ABV: _____ %

BALANCE · FINISH · DARK FRUIT · CITRUS FRUIT · FLORAL · SPICY · HERBAL/GRASSY · MALT/CEREAL · TOFFEE · PEAT · SMOKE · SWEET · SALTY · ASTRINGENT · BODY

0.1 0.2 0.3 0.4 0.5

NOTES:

....

....

....

....

....

👉 **DISTILLER:** ....

AGE/EXPRESSION: ....

ORIGIN: .... **PRICE:** ....

SAMPLED: .... **RATING:** ☆☆☆☆☆

COLOR METER:

- MAHOGANY
- CARAMEL
- AMBER
- GOLD
- HONEY
- STRAW
- CLEAR

FLAVOR WHEEL:

HEAT/ABV: _____ %

BALANCE · FINISH · DARK FRUIT · CITRUS FRUIT · FLORAL · SPICY · HERBAL/GRASSY · MALT/CEREAL · TOFFEE · PEAT · SMOKE · SWEET · SALTY · ASTRINGENT · BODY

0.5 0.4 0.3 0.2 0.1

NOTES:

....
....
....
....
....
....

DISTILLER: ....

AGE/EXPRESSION: ....

ORIGIN: .... PRICE: ....

SAMPLED: .... RATING: ☆ ☆ ☆ ☆ ☆

COLOR METER:

- MAHOGANY
- CARAMEL
- AMBER
- GOLD
- HONEY
- STRAW
- CLEAR

FLAVOR WHEEL:

HEAT/ABV: _____ %

BALANCE · FINISH · DARK FRUIT · CITRUS FRUIT · FLORAL · SPICY · HERBAL/GRASSY · MALT/CEREAL · TOFFEE · PEAT · SMOKE · SWEET · SALTY · ASTRINGENT · BODY

0.1 0.2 0.3 0.4 0.5

NOTES:

....
....
....
....
....

👉 **DISTILLER:** ....

AGE/EXPRESSION: ....

ORIGIN: .... **PRICE:** ....

SAMPLED: .... **RATING:** ☆☆☆☆☆

COLOR METER:

- MAHOGANY
- CARAMEL
- AMBER
- GOLD
- HONEY
- STRAW
- CLEAR

FLAVOR WHEEL:

HEAT/ABV: _____ %

BALANCE
FINISH
BODY
DARK FRUIT
ASTRIN-GENT
CITRUS FRUIT
SALTY
FLORAL
SWEET
SPICY
SMOKE
HERBAL/GRASSY
PEAT
TOFFEE
MALT/CEREAL

0.5
0.4
0.3
0.2
0.1

NOTES:

....

....

....

....

....

....

👉 **DISTILLER:** ....

AGE/EXPRESSION: ....

ORIGIN: .... **PRICE:** ....

SAMPLED: .... **RATING:** ☆☆☆☆☆

COLOR METER:

- MAHOGANY
- CARAMEL
- AMBER
- GOLD
- HONEY
- STRAW
- CLEAR

FLAVOR WHEEL:

HEAT/ABV: _____ %

FINISH
BALANCE
BODY
DARK FRUIT
ASTRIN-GENT
CITRUS FRUIT
SALTY
FLORAL
SWEET
SPICY
SMOKE
HERBAL/GRASSY
PEAT
TOFFEE
MALT/CEREAL

0.5
0.4
0.3
0.2
0.1

NOTES:

....
....
....
....
....
....

☞ DISTILLER: ....

AGE/EXPRESSION: ....

ORIGIN: ....   PRICE: ....

SAMPLED: ....   RATING: ☆ ☆ ☆ ☆ ☆

COLOR METER:

- MAHOGANY
- CARAMEL
- AMBER
- GOLD
- HONEY
- STRAW
- CLEAR

FLAVOR WHEEL:

HEAT/ ABV: _____ %

BALANCE
FINISH
BODY
DARK FRUIT
ASTRIN-GENT
CITRUS FRUIT
SALTY
FLORAL
SWEET
SPICY
SMOKE
HERBAL/ GRASSY
PEAT
MALT/ CEREAL
TOFFEE

0.5 0.4 0.3 0.2 0.1

NOTES:
....
....
....
....
....
....

👉 DISTILLER: ....

AGE/EXPRESSION: ....

ORIGIN: .... PRICE: ....

SAMPLED: .... RATING: ☆☆☆☆☆

COLOR METER:

- MAHOGANY
- CARAMEL
- AMBER
- GOLD
- HONEY
- STRAW
- CLEAR

FLAVOR WHEEL:

HEAT/ABV: _____ %

BALANCE
FINISH
BODY
DARK FRUIT
ASTRIN-GENT
CITRUS FRUIT
SALTY
FLORAL
SWEET
SPICY
SMOKE
HERBAL/GRASSY
PEAT
TOFFEE
MALT/CEREAL

0.5 0.4 0.3 0.2 0.1

NOTES:

....
....
....
....
....
....

👉 **DISTILLER:** ....

AGE/EXPRESSION: ....

ORIGIN: .... **PRICE:** ....

SAMPLED: .... **RATING:** ☆ ☆ ☆ ☆ ☆

COLOR METER:

- MAHOGANY
- CARAMEL
- AMBER
- GOLD
- HONEY
- STRAW
- CLEAR

FLAVOR WHEEL:

HEAT/ ABV: _____ %

BALANCE · FINISH · DARK FRUIT · CITRUS FRUIT · FLORAL · SPICY · HERBAL/GRASSY · MALT/CEREAL · TOFFEE · PEAT · SMOKE · SWEET · SALTY · ASTRIN-GENT · BODY

0.1 0.2 0.3 0.4 0.5

NOTES:

....

....

....

....

....

....

👉 **DISTILLER:** . . . .

AGE/EXPRESSION: . . . .

ORIGIN: . . . . **PRICE:** . . . .

SAMPLED: . . . . **RATING:** ☆ ☆ ☆ ☆ ☆

COLOR METER:

- MAHOGANY
- CARAMEL
- AMBER
- GOLD
- HONEY
- STRAW
- CLEAR

FLAVOR WHEEL:

HEAT/ABV : _____ %

BALANCE · FINISH · DARK FRUIT · CITRUS FRUIT · FLORAL · SPICY · HERBAL/GRASSY · MALT/CEREAL · TOFFEE · PEAT · SMOKE · SWEET · SALTY · ASTRINGENT · BODY

0.1 0.2 0.3 0.4 0.5

NOTES:

. . . .

. . . .

. . . .

. . . .

. . . .

. . . .

👉 **DISTILLER:** ....

AGE/EXPRESSION: ....

ORIGIN: .... **PRICE:** ....

SAMPLED: .... **RATING:** ☆ ☆ ☆ ☆ ☆

COLOR METER:

- MAHOGANY
- CARAMEL
- AMBER
- GOLD
- HONEY
- STRAW
- CLEAR

FLAVOR WHEEL:

HEAT/   %
ABV: _____

BALANCE   FINISH

BODY   DARK FRUIT

ASTRIN-GENT   CITRUS FRUIT

SALTY   FLORAL

SWEET   SPICY

SMOKE   HERBAL/GRASSY

PEAT   TOFFEE   MALT/CEREAL

0.5 0.4 0.3 0.2 0.1

NOTES:

....

....

....

....

....

....

DISTILLER: ....

AGE/EXPRESSION: ....

ORIGIN: ....   PRICE: ....

SAMPLED: ....   RATING: ☆ ☆ ☆ ☆ ☆

COLOR METER:

- MAHOGANY
- CARAMEL
- AMBER
- GOLD
- HONEY
- STRAW
- CLEAR

FLAVOR WHEEL:

HEAT/ABV: _____ %

BALANCE
FINISH
BODY
DARK FRUIT
ASTRINGENT
CITRUS FRUIT
SALTY
FLORAL
SWEET
SPICY
SMOKE
HERBAL/GRASSY
PEAT
TOFFEE
MALT/CEREAL

0.1 0.2 0.3 0.4 0.5

NOTES:

....

....

....

....

....

☞ **DISTILLER:** ....

AGE/EXPRESSION: ....

ORIGIN: .... **PRICE:** ....

SAMPLED: .... **RATING:** ☆ ☆ ☆ ☆ ☆

COLOR METER:

- MAHOGANY
- CARAMEL
- AMBER
- GOLD
- HONEY
- STRAW
- CLEAR

FLAVOR WHEEL:

HEAT/ %
ABV: _____

BALANCE · FINISH · DARK FRUIT
BODY · CITRUS FRUIT
ASTRIN-GENT · FLORAL
SALTY
SWEET · SPICY
SMOKE · HERBAL/GRASSY
PEAT · TOFFEE · MALT/CEREAL

0.1 0.2 0.3 0.4 0.5

NOTES:

....

....

....

....

....

....

👉 DISTILLER: ....

AGE/EXPRESSION: ....

ORIGIN: .... PRICE: ....

SAMPLED: .... RATING: ☆ ☆ ☆ ☆ ☆

COLOR METER:

- MAHOGANY
- CARAMEL
- AMBER
- GOLD
- HONEY
- STRAW
- CLEAR

FLAVOR WHEEL:

HEAT/ABV : _____ %

BALANCE FINISH DARK FRUIT
BODY CITRUS FRUIT
ASTRIN-GENT FLORAL
SALTY SPICY
SWEET HERBAL/GRASSY
SMOKE MALT/CEREAL
PEAT TOFFEE

0.5 0.4 0.3 0.2 0.1

NOTES:

....
....
....
....
....
....

👉 **DISTILLER:** ....

AGE/EXPRESSION: ....

ORIGIN: .... **PRICE:** ....

SAMPLED: .... **RATING:** ☆ ☆ ☆ ☆ ☆

COLOR METER:

- MAHOGANY
- CARAMEL
- AMBER
- GOLD
- HONEY
- STRAW
- CLEAR

FLAVOR WHEEL:

HEAT/ABV: _____ %

BALANCE   FINISH
BODY   0.5
          0.4   DARK FRUIT
ASTRIN-   0.3
GENT   0.2   CITRUS FRUIT
          0.1
SALTY   FLORAL
SWEET   SPICY
SMOKE   HERBAL/GRASSY
     SMOKE   MALT/CEREAL
  PEAT   TOFFEE

NOTES:

....

....

....

....

....

....

👉 **DISTILLER:** ....

AGE/EXPRESSION: ....

ORIGIN: .... **PRICE:** ....

SAMPLED: .... **RATING:** ☆☆☆☆☆

COLOR METER:

- MAHOGANY
- CARAMEL
- AMBER
- GOLD
- HONEY
- STRAW
- CLEAR

FLAVOR WHEEL:

HEAT/
ABV: _____ %

FINISH
BALANCE
BODY
DARK FRUIT
ASTRIN-GENT
CITRUS FRUIT
0.5
0.4
0.3
0.2
0.1
SALTY
FLORAL
SWEET
SPICY
SMOKE
HERBAL/GRASSY
PEAT
MALT/CEREAL
TOFFEE

NOTES:

....
....
....
....
....
....

DISTILLER: ....

AGE/EXPRESSION: ....

ORIGIN: .... **PRICE:** ....

SAMPLED: .... **RATING:** ☆☆☆☆☆

COLOR METER:

- MAHOGANY
- CARAMEL
- AMBER
- GOLD
- HONEY
- STRAW
- CLEAR

FLAVOR WHEEL:

HEAT/ _____ %
ABV: _____

BALANCE
FINISH
BODY
DARK FRUIT
ASTRIN-GENT
CITRUS FRUIT
SALTY
FLORAL
SWEET
SPICY
SMOKE
HERBAL/ GRASSY
PEAT
TOFFEE
MALT/ CEREAL

0.5 0.4 0.3 0.2 0.1

NOTES:

....
....
....
....
....
....

DISTILLER: ....

AGE/EXPRESSION: ....

ORIGIN: .... PRICE: ....

SAMPLED: .... RATING: ☆☆☆☆☆

COLOR METER:

- MAHOGANY
- CARAMEL
- AMBER
- GOLD
- HONEY
- STRAW
- CLEAR

FLAVOR WHEEL:

HEAT/ABV: _____ %

BALANCE · FINISH · DARK FRUIT · CITRUS FRUIT · FLORAL · SPICY · HERBAL/GRASSY · MALT/CEREAL · TOFFEE · PEAT · SMOKE · SWEET · SALTY · ASTRIN-GENT · BODY

0.1 0.2 0.3 0.4 0.5

NOTES:

....

....

....

....

....

DISTILLER: ....

AGE/EXPRESSION: ....

ORIGIN: .... **PRICE:** ....

SAMPLED: .... **RATING:** ☆ ☆ ☆ ☆ ☆

COLOR METER:

- MAHOGANY
- CARAMEL
- AMBER
- GOLD
- HONEY
- STRAW
- CLEAR

FLAVOR WHEEL:

HEAT/ABV: _____ %

BALANCE
FINISH
BODY
DARK FRUIT
ASTRIN-GENT
CITRUS FRUIT
SALTY
FLORAL
SWEET
SPICY
SMOKE
HERBAL/GRASSY
PEAT
MALT/CEREAL
TOFFEE

0.1 0.2 0.3 0.4 0.5

NOTES:

....
....
....
....
....
....

☞ **DISTILLER:** ....

AGE/EXPRESSION: ....

ORIGIN: .... **PRICE:** ....

SAMPLED: .... **RATING:** ☆☆☆☆☆

COLOR METER:

- MAHOGANY
- CARAMEL
- AMBER
- GOLD
- HONEY
- STRAW
- CLEAR

FLAVOR WHEEL:

HEAT/ABV: _____ %

BALANCE · FINISH · DARK FRUIT

BODY · CITRUS FRUIT

ASTRIN-GENT · FLORAL

SALTY · SPICY

SWEET · HERBAL/GRASSY

SMOKE · MALT/CEREAL

PEAT · TOFFEE

0.1 0.2 0.3 0.4 0.5

NOTES:

....
....
....
....
....
....

👉 **DISTILLER:** ....

AGE/EXPRESSION: ....

ORIGIN: .... **PRICE:** ....

SAMPLED: .... **RATING:** ☆☆☆☆☆

COLOR METER:

- MAHOGANY
- CARAMEL
- AMBER
- GOLD
- HONEY
- STRAW
- CLEAR

FLAVOR WHEEL:

HEAT/ABV: _____ %

BALANCE, FINISH, BODY, DARK FRUIT, ASTRINGENT, CITRUS FRUIT, SALTY, FLORAL, SWEET, SPICY, SMOKE, HERBAL/GRASSY, PEAT, MALT/CEREAL, TOFFEE

0.1 0.2 0.3 0.4 0.5

NOTES:

....
....
....
....
....
....

👉 **DISTILLER:** ....

AGE/EXPRESSION: ....

ORIGIN: .... **PRICE:** ....

SAMPLED: .... **RATING:** ☆ ☆ ☆ ☆ ☆

COLOR METER: FLAVOR WHEEL:

| HEAT/ ABV: _____ % |

MAHOGANY

CARAMEL

AMBER

GOLD

HONEY

STRAW

CLEAR

BALANCE   FINISH

BODY   DARK FRUIT

ASTRIN-   CITRUS
GENT   FRUIT

SALTY   FLORAL

SWEET   SPICY

SMOKE   HERBAL/
                               GRASSY

PEAT   TOFFEE   MALT/
                  CEREAL

0.5
0.4
0.3
0.2
0.1

NOTES:
....
....
....
....
....

DISTILLER: . . . .

AGE/EXPRESSION: . . . .

ORIGIN: . . . . **PRICE:** . . . .

SAMPLED: . . . . **RATING:** ☆ ☆ ☆ ☆ ☆

COLOR METER:

- MAHOGANY
- CARAMEL
- AMBER
- GOLD
- HONEY
- STRAW
- CLEAR

FLAVOR WHEEL:

HEAT/ABV: . . . . %

BALANCE · FINISH · DARK FRUIT · CITRUS FRUIT · FLORAL · SPICY · HERBAL/GRASSY · MALT/CEREAL · TOFFEE · PEAT · SMOKE · SWEET · SALTY · ASTRIN-GENT · BODY

0.1 0.2 0.3 0.4 0.5

NOTES:

. . . .

. . . .

. . . .

. . . .

. . . .

☞ **DISTILLER:** ....

AGE/EXPRESSION: ....

ORIGIN: .... **PRICE:** ....

SAMPLED: .... **RATING:** ☆☆☆☆☆

COLOR METER:

- MAHOGANY
- CARAMEL
- AMBER
- GOLD
- HONEY
- STRAW
- CLEAR

FLAVOR WHEEL:

HEAT/ABV : _____ %

BALANCE
FINISH
BODY
DARK FRUIT
ASTRIN-GENT
CITRUS FRUIT
SALTY
FLORAL
SWEET
SPICY
SMOKE
HERBAL/GRASSY
PEAT
TOFFEE
MALT/CEREAL

0.1 0.2 0.3 0.4 0.5

NOTES:

....
....
....
....
....

👉 **DISTILLER:** . . . .

AGE/EXPRESSION: . . . .

ORIGIN: . . . . **PRICE:** . . . .

SAMPLED: . . . . **RATING:** ☆ ☆ ☆ ☆ ☆

COLOR METER:

- MAHOGANY
- CARAMEL
- AMBER
- GOLD
- HONEY
- STRAW
- CLEAR

FLAVOR WHEEL:

HEAT/ABV: _____ %

BALANCE
FINISH
BODY
DARK FRUIT
ASTRINGENT
CITRUS FRUIT
SALTY
FLORAL
SWEET
SPICY
SMOKE
HERBAL/GRASSY
PEAT
MALT/CEREAL
TOFFEE

05
04
03
02
01

NOTES:

. . . .

. . . .

. . . .

. . . .

. . . .

. . . .

DISTILLER: . . . .

AGE/EXPRESSION: . . . .

ORIGIN: . . . .   **PRICE:** . . . .

SAMPLED: . . . .   **RATING:** ☆ ☆ ☆ ☆ ☆

COLOR METER:

- MAHOGANY
- CARAMEL
- AMBER
- GOLD
- HONEY
- STRAW
- CLEAR

FLAVOR WHEEL:

HEAT/ABV: . . . . %

BALANCE   FINISH

BODY   DARK FRUIT

ASTRIN-GENT   CITRUS FRUIT

SALTY   FLORAL

SWEET   SPICY

SMOKE   HERBAL/GRASSY

PEAT   TOFFEE   MALT/CEREAL

0.1 0.2 0.3 0.4 0.5

NOTES:

. . . .

👉 DISTILLER: ....

AGE/EXPRESSION: ....

ORIGIN: .... PRICE: ....

SAMPLED: .... RATING: ☆☆☆☆☆

COLOR METER:

- MAHOGANY
- CARAMEL
- AMBER
- GOLD
- HONEY
- STRAW
- CLEAR

FLAVOR WHEEL:

HEAT/ABV: _____ %

BALANCE · FINISH · DARK FRUIT · CITRUS FRUIT · FLORAL · SPICY · HERBAL/GRASSY · MALT/CEREAL · TOFFEE · PEAT · SMOKE · SWEET · SALTY · ASTRINGENT · BODY

0.5 0.4 0.3 0.2 0.1

NOTES:

....

....

....

....

....

....

DISTILLER: ....

AGE/EXPRESSION: ....

ORIGIN: .... **PRICE:** ....

SAMPLED: .... **RATING:** ☆ ☆ ☆ ☆ ☆

COLOR METER:

- MAHOGANY
- CARAMEL
- AMBER
- GOLD
- HONEY
- STRAW
- CLEAR

FLAVOR WHEEL:

HEAT/
ABV: _____ %

BALANCE
FINISH
BODY
DARK FRUIT
ASTRIN-GENT
CITRUS FRUIT
SALTY
FLORAL
SWEET
SPICY
SMOKE
HERBAL/GRASSY
PEAT
TOFFEE
MALT/CEREAL

0.5
0.4
0.3
0.2
0.1

NOTES:

....
....
....
....
....

☞ **DISTILLER:** ....

AGE/EXPRESSION: ....

ORIGIN: .... **PRICE:** ....

SAMPLED: .... **RATING:** ☆☆☆☆☆

COLOR METER:

- MAHOGANY
- CARAMEL
- AMBER
- GOLD
- HONEY
- STRAW
- CLEAR

FLAVOR WHEEL:

HEAT / _____ %
ABV: _____

BALANCE FINISH
BODY DARK FRUIT
ASTRIN-GENT CITRUS FRUIT
SALTY FLORAL
SWEET SPICY
SMOKE HERBAL/ GRASSY
PEAT TOFFEE MALT/ CEREAL

0.5 0.4 0.3 0.2 0.1

NOTES:
....
....
....
....
....
....

DISTILLER: ....

AGE/EXPRESSION: ....

ORIGIN: .... **PRICE:** ....

SAMPLED: .... **RATING:** ☆ ☆ ☆ ☆ ☆

COLOR METER:

- MAHOGANY
- CARAMEL
- AMBER
- GOLD
- HONEY
- STRAW
- CLEAR

FLAVOR WHEEL:

HEAT/ABV: _____ %

BALANCE
FINISH
BODY
DARK FRUIT
ASTRIN-GENT
CITRUS FRUIT
SALTY
FLORAL
SWEET
SPICY
SMOKE
HERBAL/GRASSY
PEAT
TOFFEE
MALT/CEREAL

0.1 0.2 0.3 0.4 0.5

NOTES:

....
....
....
....
....
....

👉 **DISTILLER:** ....

AGE/EXPRESSION: ....

ORIGIN: .... **PRICE:** ....

SAMPLED: .... **RATING:** ☆ ☆ ☆ ☆ ☆

COLOR METER:

- MAHOGANY
- CARAMEL
- AMBER
- GOLD
- HONEY
- STRAW
- CLEAR

FLAVOR WHEEL:

HEAT / .... %
ABV : ....

BALANCE   FINISH

BODY

DARK FRUIT

ASTRIN-GENT

CITRUS FRUIT

SALTY

FLORAL

SWEET

SPICY

SMOKE

HERBAL/ GRASSY

PEAT   TOFFEE   MALT/ CEREAL

0.5
0.4
0.3
0.2
0.1

NOTES:
....
....
....
....
....

☞ **DISTILLER:** ....

AGE/EXPRESSION: ....

ORIGIN: .... **PRICE:** ....

SAMPLED: .... **RATING:** ☆ ☆ ☆ ☆ ☆

COLOR METER:

- MAHOGANY
- CARAMEL
- AMBER
- GOLD
- HONEY
- STRAW
- CLEAR

FLAVOR WHEEL:

HEAT / ABV: _____ %

BALANCE
FINISH
BODY
ASTRIN- GENT
DARK FRUIT
CITRUS FRUIT
SALTY
FLORAL
SWEET
SPICY
SMOKE
HERBAL/ GRASSY
PEAT
TOFFEE
MALT/ CEREAL

0.5 0.4 0.3 0.2 0.1

NOTES: ....
....
....
....
....
....

👉 **DISTILLER:** ....

AGE/EXPRESSION: ....

ORIGIN: .... **PRICE:** ....

SAMPLED: .... **RATING:** ☆☆☆☆☆

COLOR METER:

- MAHOGANY
- CARAMEL
- AMBER
- GOLD
- HONEY
- STRAW
- CLEAR

FLAVOR WHEEL:

HEAT / ABV : _____ %

BALANCE FINISH

BODY DARK FRUIT

ASTRIN-GENT CITRUS FRUIT

SALTY FLORAL

SWEET SPICY

SMOKE HERBAL/GRASSY

PEAT TOFFEE MALT/CEREAL

0.5 0.4 0.3 0.2 0.1

NOTES:

....
....
....
....
....
....

DISTILLER: ....

AGE/EXPRESSION: ....

ORIGIN: .... **PRICE:** ....

SAMPLED: .... **RATING:** ☆ ☆ ☆ ☆ ☆

COLOR METER:

- MAHOGANY
- CARAMEL
- AMBER
- GOLD
- HONEY
- STRAW
- CLEAR

FLAVOR WHEEL:

HEAT/ ABV: _____ %

BALANCE   FINISH
BODY   DARK FRUIT
ASTRIN-GENT   CITRUS FRUIT
SALTY   FLORAL
SWEET   SPICY
SMOKE   HERBAL/ GRASSY
PEAT   TOFFEE   MALT/ CEREAL

05 04 03 02 01

NOTES:

....
....
....
....
....

👉 **DISTILLER:** . . . .

AGE/EXPRESSION: . . . .

ORIGIN: . . . . **PRICE:** . . . .

SAMPLED: . . . . **RATING:** ☆ ☆ ☆ ☆ ☆

COLOR METER:

- MAHOGANY
- CARAMEL
- AMBER
- GOLD
- HONEY
- STRAW
- CLEAR

FLAVOR WHEEL:

HEAT/ABV : . . . . %

BALANCE · FINISH · DARK FRUIT · CITRUS FRUIT · FLORAL · SPICY · HERBAL/GRASSY · MALT/CEREAL · TOFFEE · PEAT · SMOKE · SWEET · SALTY · ASTRINGENT · BODY

0.5 0.4 0.3 0.2 0.1

NOTES: . . . .

. . . .

. . . .

. . . .

. . . .

. . . .

☞ **DISTILLER:** ....

AGE/EXPRESSION: ....

ORIGIN: .... **PRICE:** ....

SAMPLED: .... **RATING:** ☆☆☆☆☆

COLOR METER:

- MAHOGANY
- CARAMEL
- AMBER
- GOLD
- HONEY
- STRAW
- CLEAR

FLAVOR WHEEL:

HEAT/ABV: _____ %

BALANCE
BODY
FINISH
ASTRINGENT
SALTY
SWEET
SMOKE
PEAT
TOFFEE
MALT/CEREAL
HERBAL/GRASSY
SPICY
FLORAL
CITRUS FRUIT
DARK FRUIT

0.1 0.2 0.3 0.4 0.5

NOTES: ....
....
....
....
....
....

👉 **DISTILLER:** ....

AGE/EXPRESSION: ....

ORIGIN: .... **PRICE:** ....

SAMPLED: .... **RATING:** ☆ ☆ ☆ ☆ ☆

COLOR METER:

- MAHOGANY
- CARAMEL
- AMBER
- GOLD
- HONEY
- STRAW
- CLEAR

FLAVOR WHEEL:

HEAT/ABV: _____ %

FINISH
BALANCE
BODY
DARK FRUIT
ASTRIN-GENT
CITRUS FRUIT
SALTY
FLORAL
SWEET
SPICY
SMOKE
HERBAL/GRASSY
PEAT
TOFFEE
MALT/CEREAL

0.1 0.2 0.3 0.4 0.5

NOTES: ....
....
....
....
....
....

DISTILLER: ....

AGE/EXPRESSION: ....

ORIGIN: .... **PRICE:** ....

SAMPLED: .... **RATING:** ☆☆☆☆☆

COLOR METER:

- MAHOGANY
- CARAMEL
- AMBER
- GOLD
- HONEY
- STRAW
- CLEAR

FLAVOR WHEEL:

HEAT/ ABV: _____ %

BALANCE · FINISH · DARK FRUIT · CITRUS FRUIT · FLORAL · SPICY · HERBAL/GRASSY · MALT/CEREAL · TOFFEE · PEAT · SMOKE · SWEET · SALTY · ASTRINGENT · BODY

0.5 0.4 0.3 0.2 0.1

NOTES:

....

....

....

....

....

....

👉 **DISTILLER:** ....

AGE/EXPRESSION: ....

ORIGIN: .... **PRICE:** ....

SAMPLED: .... **RATING:** ☆☆☆☆☆

COLOR METER:

- MAHOGANY
- CARAMEL
- AMBER
- GOLD
- HONEY
- STRAW
- CLEAR

FLAVOR WHEEL:

HEAT/ABV: _____ %

BALANCE
FINISH
BODY
DARK FRUIT
ASTRIN-GENT
CITRUS FRUIT
SALTY
FLORAL
SWEET
SPICY
SMOKE
HERBAL/GRASSY
PEAT
TOFFEE
MALT/CEREAL

0.5 0.4 0.3 0.2 0.1

NOTES:
....
....
....
....
....
....

👉 **DISTILLER:** ....

AGE/EXPRESSION: ....

ORIGIN: .... **PRICE:** ....

SAMPLED: .... **RATING:** ☆☆☆☆☆

COLOR METER:

MAHOGANY

CARAMEL

AMBER

GOLD

HONEY

STRAW

CLEAR

FLAVOR WHEEL:

HEAT/ABV: _____ %

BALANCE
FINISH
BODY
DARK FRUIT
ASTRIN-GENT
CITRUS FRUIT
SALTY
FLORAL
SWEET
SPICY
SMOKE
HERBAL/GRASSY
PEAT
TOFFEE
MALT/CEREAL

05
04
03
02
01

NOTES:

....

....

....

....

....

👉 **DISTILLER:** ....

AGE/EXPRESSION: ....

ORIGIN: .... **PRICE:** ....

SAMPLED: .... **RATING:** ☆☆☆☆☆

COLOR METER:

- MAHOGANY
- CARAMEL
- AMBER
- GOLD
- HONEY
- STRAW
- CLEAR

FLAVOR WHEEL:

HEAT / %
ABV : _____

BALANCE   FINISH
BODY   DARK FRUIT
ASTRIN-   CITRUS
GENT   FRUIT
SALTY   FLORAL
SWEET   SPICY
SMOKE   HERBAL/
                   GRASSY
PEAT   TOFFEE   MALT/
                 CEREAL

0.5
0.4
0.3
0.2
0.1

NOTES:

....
....
....
....
....
....

☞ **DISTILLER:** ....

AGE/EXPRESSION: ....

ORIGIN: .... **PRICE:** ....

SAMPLED: .... **RATING:** ☆☆☆☆☆

COLOR METER:

- MAHOGANY
- CARAMEL
- AMBER
- GOLD
- HONEY
- STRAW
- CLEAR

FLAVOR WHEEL:

HEAT/ABV: _____ %

BALANCE · FINISH · DARK FRUIT
BODY · CITRUS FRUIT
ASTRIN-GENT · FLORAL
SALTY
SWEET · SPICY
SMOKE · HERBAL/GRASSY
PEAT · TOFFEE · MALT/CEREAL

0.1 · 0.2 · 0.3 · 0.4 · 0.5

NOTES:

....
....
....
....
....
....

DISTILLER: ....

AGE/EXPRESSION: ....

ORIGIN: .... **PRICE:** ....

SAMPLED: .... **RATING:** ☆ ☆ ☆ ☆ ☆

COLOR METER:

- MAHOGANY
- CARAMEL
- AMBER
- GOLD
- HONEY
- STRAW
- CLEAR

FLAVOR WHEEL:

HEAT/ABV: _____ %

BALANCE · FINISH · DARK FRUIT · CITRUS FRUIT · FLORAL · SPICY · HERBAL/GRASSY · MALT/CEREAL · TOFFEE · PEAT · SMOKE · SWEET · SALTY · ASTRINGENT · BODY

0.1 0.2 0.3 0.4 0.5

NOTES:

....
....
....
....
....
....

👉 **DISTILLER:** ....

AGE/EXPRESSION: ....

ORIGIN: .... **PRICE:** ....

SAMPLED: .... **RATING:** ☆ ☆ ☆ ☆ ☆

COLOR METER:

- MAHOGANY
- CARAMEL
- AMBER
- GOLD
- HONEY
- STRAW
- CLEAR

FLAVOR WHEEL:

BALANCE FINISH

BODY

ASTRIN-GENT

SALTY

SWEET

SMOKE

PEAT TOFFEE MALT/CEREAL

HERBAL/GRASSY

SPICY

FLORAL

CITRUS FRUIT

DARK FRUIT

HEAT/ABV: _____ %

0.5 0.4 0.3 0.2 0.1

NOTES:

....

....

....

....

....

....

👉 **DISTILLER:** ....

AGE/EXPRESSION: ....

ORIGIN: .... **PRICE:** ....

SAMPLED: .... **RATING:** ☆☆☆☆☆

COLOR METER:

- MAHOGANY
- CARAMEL
- AMBER
- GOLD
- HONEY
- STRAW
- CLEAR

FLAVOR WHEEL:

HEAT/ABV: _____ %

BALANCE
FINISH
BODY
DARK FRUIT
ASTRIN-GENT
CITRUS FRUIT
SALTY
FLORAL
SWEET
SPICY
SMOKE
HERBAL/GRASSY
PEAT
TOFFEE
MALT/CEREAL

0.5
0.4
0.3
0.2
0.1

NOTES: ....

....

....

....

....

....

DISTILLER: ....

AGE/EXPRESSION: ....

ORIGIN: .... **PRICE:** ....

SAMPLED: .... **RATING:** ☆ ☆ ☆ ☆ ☆

COLOR METER:

- MAHOGANY
- CARAMEL
- AMBER
- GOLD
- HONEY
- STRAW
- CLEAR

FLAVOR WHEEL:

HEAT/ABV: _____ %

BALANCE, FINISH, BODY, DARK FRUIT, ASTRIN-GENT, CITRUS FRUIT, SALTY, FLORAL, SWEET, SPICY, SMOKE, HERBAL/GRASSY, PEAT, TOFFEE, MALT/CEREAL

0.1 0.2 0.3 0.4 0.5

NOTES:

....

....

....

....

....

....

👉 **DISTILLER:** ....

AGE/EXPRESSION: ....

ORIGIN: .... **PRICE:** ....

SAMPLED: .... **RATING:** ☆☆☆☆☆

COLOR METER:

- MAHOGANY
- CARAMEL
- AMBER
- GOLD
- HONEY
- STRAW
- CLEAR

FLAVOR WHEEL:

HEAT/ ABV : _____ %

BALANCE · FINISH · DARK FRUIT · CITRUS FRUIT · FLORAL · SPICY · HERBAL/GRASSY · MALT/CEREAL · TOFFEE · PEAT · SMOKE · SWEET · SALTY · ASTRINGENT · BODY

0.1 0.2 0.3 0.4 0.5

NOTES:
....
....
....
....
....
....

👉 **DISTILLER:** ....

AGE/EXPRESSION: ....

ORIGIN: .... **PRICE:** ....

SAMPLED: .... **RATING:** ☆☆☆☆☆

COLOR METER:

- MAHOGANY
- CARAMEL
- AMBER
- GOLD
- HONEY
- STRAW
- CLEAR

FLAVOR WHEEL:

HEAT/ABV: _____ %

BALANCE
FINISH
BODY
DARK FRUIT
ASTRIN-GENT
CITRUS FRUIT
SALTY
FLORAL
SWEET
SPICY
SMOKE
HERBAL/GRASSY
PEAT
TOFFEE
MALT/CEREAL

0.1 0.2 0.3 0.4 0.5

NOTES:
....
....
....
....
....
....

☞ **DISTILLER:** ....

AGE/EXPRESSION: ....

ORIGIN: .... **PRICE:** ....

SAMPLED: .... **RATING:** ☆☆☆☆☆

COLOR METER:

MAHOGANY

CARAMEL

AMBER

GOLD

HONEY

STRAW

CLEAR

FLAVOR WHEEL:

BALANCE · FINISH

BODY · DARK FRUIT

ASTRIN-GENT · CITRUS FRUIT

SALTY · FLORAL

SWEET · SPICY

SMOKE · HERBAL/GRASSY

PEAT · TOFFEE · MALT/CEREAL

0.5 0.4 0.3 0.2 0.1

HEAT/ABV: _____ %

NOTES: ....

....

....

....

....

....

👉 **DISTILLER:** ....

AGE/EXPRESSION: ....

ORIGIN: .... **PRICE:** ....

SAMPLED: .... **RATING:** ☆☆☆☆☆

COLOR METER:

- MAHOGANY
- CARAMEL
- AMBER
- GOLD
- HONEY
- STRAW
- CLEAR

FLAVOR WHEEL:

HEAT/ABV: _____ %

BALANCE · FINISH · DARK FRUIT · BODY · ASTRINGENT · CITRUS FRUIT · SALTY · FLORAL · SWEET · SPICY · SMOKE · HERBAL/GRASSY · PEAT · TOFFEE · MALT/CEREAL

0.5 0.4 0.3 0.2 0.1

NOTES:

....

....

....

....

....

👉 **DISTILLER:** ....

AGE/EXPRESSION: ....

ORIGIN: .... **PRICE:** ....

SAMPLED: .... **RATING:** ☆☆☆☆☆

COLOR METER:

- MAHOGANY
- CARAMEL
- AMBER
- GOLD
- HONEY
- STRAW
- CLEAR

FLAVOR WHEEL:

HEAT/
ABV: _____ %

BALANCE
FINISH
BODY
DARK FRUIT
ASTRIN-GENT
CITRUS FRUIT
SALTY
FLORAL
SWEET
SPICY
SMOKE
HERBAL/GRASSY
PEAT
TOFFEE
MALT/CEREAL

0.5
0.4
0.3
0.2
0.1

NOTES: ....
....
....
....
....
....

DISTILLER: ....

AGE/EXPRESSION: ....

ORIGIN: .... **PRICE:** ....

SAMPLED: .... **RATING:** ☆☆☆☆☆

COLOR METER:

- MAHOGANY
- CARAMEL
- AMBER
- GOLD
- HONEY
- STRAW
- CLEAR

FLAVOR WHEEL:

HEAT/ABV: _____ %

BALANCE · FINISH
BODY · DARK FRUIT
ASTRINGENT · CITRUS FRUIT
SALTY · FLORAL
SWEET · SPICY
SMOKE · HERBAL/GRASSY
PEAT · TOFFEE · MALT/CEREAL

0.1 0.2 0.3 0.4 0.5

NOTES:

....
....
....
....
....
....

DISTILLER: ....

AGE/EXPRESSION: ....

ORIGIN: .... PRICE: ....

SAMPLED: .... RATING: ☆ ☆ ☆ ☆ ☆

COLOR METER:

- MAHOGANY
- CARAMEL
- AMBER
- GOLD
- HONEY
- STRAW
- CLEAR

FLAVOR WHEEL:

HEAT / ABV: _____ %

BALANCE · FINISH · BODY · DARK FRUIT · CITRUS FRUIT · ASTRINGENT · FLORAL · SALTY · SPICY · SWEET · HERBAL/GRASSY · SMOKE · MALT/CEREAL · PEAT · TOFFEE

0.5 0.4 0.3 0.2 0.1

NOTES:

....
....
....
....
....
....

DISTILLER: ....

AGE/EXPRESSION: ....

ORIGIN: .... **PRICE:** ....

SAMPLED: .... **RATING:** ☆☆☆☆☆

COLOR METER:

- MAHOGANY
- CARAMEL
- AMBER
- GOLD
- HONEY
- STRAW
- CLEAR

FLAVOR WHEEL:

HEAT/ABV: _____ %

BALANCE, FINISH, BODY, DARK FRUIT, ASTRIN-GENT, CITRUS FRUIT, SALTY, FLORAL, SWEET, SPICY, SMOKE, HERBAL/GRASSY, PEAT, TOFFEE, MALT/CEREAL

0.5, 0.4, 0.3, 0.2, 0.1

NOTES:
....
....
....
....
....
....

👉 **DISTILLER:** ....

AGE/EXPRESSION: ....

ORIGIN: .... **PRICE:** ....

SAMPLED: .... **RATING:** ☆☆☆☆☆

COLOR METER:

- MAHOGANY
- CARAMEL
- AMBER
- GOLD
- HONEY
- STRAW
- CLEAR

FLAVOR WHEEL:

HEAT/ABV: _____ %

BALANCE
FINISH
BODY
DARK FRUIT
ASTRIN-GENT
CITRUS FRUIT
SALTY
FLORAL
SWEET
SPICY
SMOKE
HERBAL/GRASSY
PEAT
TOFFEE
MALT/CEREAL

0.1 0.2 0.3 0.4 0.5

NOTES: ....
....
....
....
....
....
....

👉 DISTILLER: ....

AGE/EXPRESSION: ....

ORIGIN: .... PRICE: ....

SAMPLED: .... RATING: ☆ ☆ ☆ ☆ ☆

COLOR METER:

MAHOGANY

CARAMEL

AMBER

GOLD

HONEY

STRAW

CLEAR

FLAVOR WHEEL:

HEAT/ %
ABV: _____

BALANCE   FINISH
BODY   DARK FRUIT
ASTRIN-   CITRUS
GENT   FRUIT
SALTY   FLORAL
SWEET   SPICY
SMOKE   HERBAL/
                        GRASSY
PEAT   TOFFEE   MALT/
                CEREAL

0.5
0.4
0.3
0.2
0.1

NOTES:

....

....

....

....

....

....

👉 **DISTILLER:** ....

AGE/EXPRESSION: ....

ORIGIN: .... **PRICE:** ....

SAMPLED: .... **RATING:** ☆☆☆☆☆

COLOR METER:

- MAHOGANY
- CARAMEL
- AMBER
- GOLD
- HONEY
- STRAW
- CLEAR

FLAVOR WHEEL:

HEAT/ABV : _____ %

BALANCE · FINISH · BODY · DARK FRUIT · ASTRINGENT · CITRUS FRUIT · SALTY · FLORAL · SWEET · SPICY · SMOKE · HERBAL/GRASSY · PEAT · TOFFEE · MALT/CEREAL

0.1 0.2 0.3 0.4 0.5

NOTES: ....
....
....
....
....
....

👉 **DISTILLER:** ....

AGE/EXPRESSION: ....

ORIGIN: .... **PRICE:** ....

SAMPLED: .... **RATING:** ☆☆☆☆☆

COLOR METER:

- MAHOGANY
- CARAMEL
- AMBER
- GOLD
- HONEY
- STRAW
- CLEAR

FLAVOR WHEEL:

HEAT/ABV: _____ %

BALANCE
FINISH
BODY
DARK FRUIT
ASTRIN-GENT
CITRUS FRUIT
SALTY
FLORAL
SWEET
SPICY
SMOKE
HERBAL/GRASSY
PEAT
TOFFEE
MALT/CEREAL

5 4 3 2 1

NOTES:

....

....

....

....

....

👉 **DISTILLER:** ....

AGE/EXPRESSION: ....

ORIGIN: .... **PRICE:** ....

SAMPLED: .... **RATING:** ☆☆☆☆☆

COLOR METER:

- MAHOGANY
- CARAMEL
- AMBER
- GOLD
- HONEY
- STRAW
- CLEAR

FLAVOR WHEEL:

HEAT/ABV: _____ %

BALANCE · FINISH · DARK FRUIT · CITRUS FRUIT · FLORAL · SPICY · HERBAL/GRASSY · MALT/CEREAL · TOFFEE · PEAT · SMOKE · SWEET · SALTY · ASTRINGENT · BODY

0.5 0.4 0.3 0.2 0.1

NOTES:

....
....
....
....
....
....

DISTILLER: ....

AGE/EXPRESSION: ....

ORIGIN: .... **PRICE:** ....

SAMPLED: .... **RATING:** ☆☆☆☆☆

COLOR METER:

- MAHOGANY
- CARAMEL
- AMBER
- GOLD
- HONEY
- STRAW
- CLEAR

FLAVOR WHEEL:

HEAT/ABV: _____ %

BALANCE · FINISH · BODY · DARK FRUIT · ASTRINGENT · CITRUS FRUIT · SALTY · FLORAL · SWEET · SPICY · SMOKE · HERBAL/GRASSY · PEAT · TOFFEE · MALT/CEREAL

5 4 3 2 1

NOTES:

....
....
....
....
....

👉 **DISTILLER:** ....

AGE/EXPRESSION: ....

ORIGIN: .... **PRICE:** ....

SAMPLED: .... **RATING:** ☆☆☆☆☆

COLOR METER:

- MAHOGANY
- CARAMEL
- AMBER
- GOLD
- HONEY
- STRAW
- CLEAR

FLAVOR WHEEL:

HEAT/ABV: _____ %

BALANCE
FINISH
BODY
DARK FRUIT
ASTRIN-GENT
CITRUS FRUIT
SALTY
FLORAL
SWEET
SPICY
SMOKE
HERBAL/GRASSY
PEAT
TOFFEE
MALT/CEREAL

0.1 0.2 0.3 0.4 0.5

NOTES:
....
....
....
....
....
....

DISTILLER: . . . .

AGE/EXPRESSION: . . . .

ORIGIN: . . . . **PRICE:** . . . .

SAMPLED: . . . . **RATING:** ☆ ☆ ☆ ☆ ☆

COLOR METER:

- MAHOGANY
- CARAMEL
- AMBER
- GOLD
- HONEY
- STRAW
- CLEAR

FLAVOR WHEEL:

HEAT/ABV: _____ %

BALANCE · FINISH · DARK FRUIT · CITRUS FRUIT · FLORAL · SPICY · HERBAL/GRASSY · MALT/CEREAL · TOFFEE · PEAT · SMOKE · SWEET · SALTY · ASTRINGENT · BODY

0.5 0.4 0.3 0.2 0.1

NOTES:

. . . .

. . . .

. . . .

. . . .

. . . .

👉 **DISTILLER:** ....

AGE/EXPRESSION: ....

ORIGIN: .... **PRICE:** ....

SAMPLED: .... **RATING:** ☆☆☆☆☆

COLOR METER:

- MAHOGANY
- CARAMEL
- AMBER
- GOLD
- HONEY
- STRAW
- CLEAR

FLAVOR WHEEL:

HEAT/ABV: _____ %

BALANCE · FINISH · DARK FRUIT · CITRUS FRUIT · FLORAL · SPICY · HERBAL/GRASSY · MALT/CEREAL · TOFFEE · PEAT · SMOKE · SWEET · SALTY · ASTRINGENT · BODY

0.5
0.4
0.3
0.2
0.1

NOTES:

....

....

....

....

....

....

DISTILLER: ....

AGE/EXPRESSION: ....

ORIGIN: .... **PRICE:** ....

SAMPLED: .... **RATING:** ☆☆☆☆☆

COLOR METER:

- MAHOGANY
- CARAMEL
- AMBER
- GOLD
- HONEY
- STRAW
- CLEAR

FLAVOR WHEEL:

HEAT/ABV: _____ %

BALANCE · FINISH · BODY · DARK FRUIT · ASTRINGENT · CITRUS FRUIT · SALTY · FLORAL · SWEET · SPICY · SMOKE · HERBAL/GRASSY · PEAT · TOFFEE · MALT/CEREAL

NOTES:

....
....
....
....
....
....

👉 DISTILLER: ....

AGE/EXPRESSION: ....

ORIGIN: .... PRICE: ....

SAMPLED: .... RATING: ☆☆☆☆☆

COLOR METER:

- MAHOGANY
- CARAMEL
- AMBER
- GOLD
- HONEY
- STRAW
- CLEAR

FLAVOR WHEEL:

HEAT/ _____ %
ABV: _____

BALANCE · FINISH
BODY · DARK FRUIT
ASTRIN-GENT · CITRUS FRUIT
SALTY · FLORAL
SWEET · SPICY
SMOKE · HERBAL/GRASSY
PEAT · TOFFEE · MALT/CEREAL

0.5
0.4
0.3
0.2
0.1

NOTES:

....
....
....
....
....
....

👉 **DISTILLER:** . . . .

AGE/EXPRESSION: . . . .

ORIGIN: . . . . **PRICE:** . . . .

SAMPLED: . . . . **RATING:** ☆ ☆ ☆ ☆ ☆

COLOR METER:

- MAHOGANY
- CARAMEL
- AMBER
- GOLD
- HONEY
- STRAW
- CLEAR

FLAVOR WHEEL:

HEAT/ _____ %
ABV: _____

BALANCE · FINISH
BODY
ASTRIN-GENT
SALTY · DARK FRUIT
SWEET · CITRUS FRUIT
SMOKE · FLORAL
PEAT · SPICY
TOFFEE · HERBAL/GRASSY
MALT/CEREAL

0.5 0.4 0.3 0.2 0.1

NOTES: . . . .

. . . .

. . . .

. . . .

. . . .

. . . .

👉 **DISTILLER:** ....

AGE/EXPRESSION: ....

ORIGIN: .... **PRICE:** ....

SAMPLED: .... **RATING:** ☆☆☆☆☆

COLOR METER:

- MAHOGANY
- CARAMEL
- AMBER
- GOLD
- HONEY
- STRAW
- CLEAR

FLAVOR WHEEL:

HEAT/ABV: _____ %

BALANCE · FINISH
BODY · DARK FRUIT
ASTRINGENT · CITRUS FRUIT
SALTY · FLORAL
SWEET · SPICY
SMOKE · HERBAL/GRASSY
PEAT · TOFFEE · MALT/CEREAL

0.5 0.4 0.3 0.2 0.1

NOTES: ....
....
....
....
....
....

👉 **DISTILLER:** ....

AGE/EXPRESSION: ....

ORIGIN: .... **PRICE:** ....

SAMPLED: .... **RATING:** ☆ ☆ ☆ ☆ ☆

COLOR METER:

- MAHOGANY
- CARAMEL
- AMBER
- GOLD
- HONEY
- STRAW
- CLEAR

FLAVOR WHEEL:

HEAT/ %
ABV: _____

BALANCE
FINISH
BODY
DARK FRUIT
ASTRIN-GENT
CITRUS FRUIT
SALTY
FLORAL
SWEET
SPICY
SMOKE
HERBAL/GRASSY
PEAT
TOFFEE
MALT/CEREAL

0.5 0.4 0.3 0.2 0.1

NOTES:

....

....

....

....

....

....

👉 **DISTILLER:** ....

AGE/EXPRESSION: ....

ORIGIN: .... **PRICE:** ....

SAMPLED: .... **RATING:** ☆ ☆ ☆ ☆ ☆

COLOR METER:

- MAHOGANY
- CARAMEL
- AMBER
- GOLD
- HONEY
- STRAW
- CLEAR

FLAVOR WHEEL:

HEAT/ABV : _____ %

BALANCE
FINISH
BODY
DARK FRUIT
ASTRIN-GENT
CITRUS FRUIT
SALTY
FLORAL
SWEET
SPICY
SMOKE
HERBAL/GRASSY
PEAT
MALT/CEREAL
TOFFEE

0.5
0.4
0.3
0.2
0.1

NOTES:

....
....
....
....
....
....

DISTILLER: ....

AGE/EXPRESSION: ....

ORIGIN: .... PRICE: ....

SAMPLED: .... RATING: ☆☆☆☆☆

COLOR METER:

MAHOGANY

CARAMEL

AMBER

GOLD

HONEY

STRAW

CLEAR

FLAVOR WHEEL:

HEAT/   %
ABV: _____

BALANCE   FINISH

BODY   DARK FRUIT

ASTRIN-   CITRUS
GENT   FRUIT

SALTY   FLORAL

SWEET   SPICY

SMOKE   HERBAL/
                        GRASSY

PEAT   TOFFEE   MALT/
               CEREAL

0.5
0.4
0.3
0.2
0.1

NOTES: ....
....
....
....
....
....

👉 **DISTILLER:** ....

AGE/EXPRESSION: ....

ORIGIN: .... **PRICE:** ....

SAMPLED: .... **RATING:** ☆ ☆ ☆ ☆ ☆

COLOR METER:

- MAHOGANY
- CARAMEL
- AMBER
- GOLD
- HONEY
- STRAW
- CLEAR

FLAVOR WHEEL:

BALANCE   FINISH

BODY

HEAT/   %
ABV: _____

ASTRIN-
GENT   DARK FRUIT

SALTY   CITRUS
                                  FRUIT

SWEET   FLORAL

SMOKE   SPICY

PEAT   TOFFEE   MALT/   HERBAL/
                CEREAL   GRASSY

0.5
0.4
0.3
0.2
0.1

NOTES:
....
....
....
....
....
....

👉 **DISTILLER:** ....

AGE/EXPRESSION: ....

ORIGIN: .... **PRICE:** ....

SAMPLED: .... **RATING:** ☆☆☆☆☆

COLOR METER:

- MAHOGANY
- CARAMEL
- AMBER
- GOLD
- HONEY
- STRAW
- CLEAR

FLAVOR WHEEL:

HEAT/ABV: _____ %

BALANCE — FINISH — DARK FRUIT
BODY — CITRUS FRUIT
ASTRINGENT — 0.5 0.4 0.3 0.2 0.1 — FLORAL
SALTY
SWEET — SPICY
SMOKE — HERBAL/GRASSY
PEAT — TOFFEE — MALT/CEREAL

NOTES:

....
....
....
....
....
....

👉 **DISTILLER:** . . . .

AGE/EXPRESSION: . . . .

ORIGIN: . . . . **PRICE:** . . . .

SAMPLED: . . . . **RATING:** ☆ ☆ ☆ ☆ ☆

COLOR METER:

MAHOGANY

CARAMEL

AMBER

GOLD

HONEY

STRAW

CLEAR

FLAVOR WHEEL:

HEAT/ . . . . %
ABV: . . . .

BALANCE   FINISH

BODY   DARK FRUIT

ASTRIN-   CITRUS
GENT   FRUIT

SALTY   FLORAL

SWEET   SPICY

SMOKE   HERBAL/
                   GRASSY

PEAT   TOFFEE   MALT/
                 CEREAL

0.5
0.4
0.3
0.2
0.1

NOTES: . . . .
. . . .
. . . .
. . . .
. . . .
. . . .

DISTILLER: ....

AGE/EXPRESSION: ....

ORIGIN: .... PRICE: ....

SAMPLED: .... RATING: ☆ ☆ ☆ ☆ ☆

COLOR METER:

- MAHOGANY
- CARAMEL
- AMBER
- GOLD
- HONEY
- STRAW
- CLEAR

FLAVOR WHEEL:

HEAT/
ABV: _____ %

BALANCE
BODY
FINISH
ASTRIN-GENT
SALTY
SWEET
SMOKE
PEAT
TOFFEE
MALT/CEREAL
HERBAL/GRASSY
SPICY
FLORAL
CITRUS FRUIT
DARK FRUIT

0.1 0.2 0.3 0.4 0.5

NOTES:

....
....
....
....
....
....

👉 **DISTILLER:** ....

AGE/EXPRESSION: ....

ORIGIN: .... **PRICE:** ....

SAMPLED: .... **RATING:** ☆ ☆ ☆ ☆ ☆

COLOR METER:

- MAHOGANY
- CARAMEL
- AMBER
- GOLD
- HONEY
- STRAW
- CLEAR

FLAVOR WHEEL:

HEAT / ABV : _____ %

BALANCE · FINISH · DARK FRUIT · CITRUS FRUIT · FLORAL · SPICY · HERBAL/GRASSY · MALT/CEREAL · TOFFEE · PEAT · SMOKE · SWEET · SALTY · ASTRIN-GENT · BODY

0.5 0.4 0.3 0.2 0.1

NOTES: ....
....
....
....
....
....

DISTILLER: ....

AGE/EXPRESSION: ....

ORIGIN: .... PRICE: ....

SAMPLED: .... RATING: ☆☆☆☆☆

COLOR METER:

- MAHOGANY
- CARAMEL
- AMBER
- GOLD
- HONEY
- STRAW
- CLEAR

FLAVOR WHEEL:

HEAT/ _____%
ABV: _____

BALANCE   FINISH

BODY   DARK FRUIT

ASTRIN-   CITRUS
GENT   FRUIT

SALTY   FLORAL

SWEET   SPICY

SMOKE   HERBAL/
                       GRASSY

PEAT   TOFFEE   MALT/
                 CEREAL

0.5
0.4
0.3
0.2
0.1

NOTES:
....
....
....
....
....
....

👉 **DISTILLER:** ....

AGE/EXPRESSION: ....

ORIGIN: .... **PRICE:** ....

SAMPLED: .... **RATING:** ☆☆☆☆☆

COLOR METER: FLAVOR WHEEL:

- MAHOGANY
- CARAMEL
- AMBER
- GOLD
- HONEY
- STRAW
- CLEAR

HEAT/ABV: _____ %

BALANCE   FINISH

BODY   DARK FRUIT

ASTRIN-   CITRUS
GENT   FRUIT

SALTY   FLORAL

SWEET   SPICY

SMOKE   HERBAL/
                          GRASSY

PEAT   TOFFEE   MALT/
                  CEREAL

0.5
0.4
0.3
0.2
0.1

NOTES: ....
....
....
....
....
....

👉 **DISTILLER:** ....

AGE/EXPRESSION: ....

ORIGIN: .... **PRICE:** ....

SAMPLED: .... **RATING:** ☆☆☆☆☆

COLOR METER:

- MAHOGANY
- CARAMEL
- AMBER
- GOLD
- HONEY
- STRAW
- CLEAR

FLAVOR WHEEL:

HEAT/ABV: _____ %

BALANCE · FINISH · DARK FRUIT · CITRUS FRUIT · FLORAL · SPICY · HERBAL/GRASSY · MALT/CEREAL · TOFFEE · PEAT · SMOKE · SWEET · SALTY · ASTRINGENT · BODY

0.1 0.2 0.3 0.4 0.5

NOTES:

....

....

....

....

....

....

☞ **DISTILLER:** . . . .

AGE/EXPRESSION: . . . .

ORIGIN: . . . . **PRICE:** . . . .

SAMPLED: . . . . **RATING:** ☆☆☆☆☆

COLOR METER:

- MAHOGANY
- CARAMEL
- AMBER
- GOLD
- HONEY
- STRAW
- CLEAR

FLAVOR WHEEL:

HEAT/ABV: . . . . %

BALANCE • FINISH • DARK FRUIT • CITRUS FRUIT • FLORAL • SPICY • HERBAL/GRASSY • MALT/CEREAL • TOFFEE • PEAT • SMOKE • SWEET • SALTY • ASTRINGENT • BODY

0.1 0.2 0.3 0.4 0.5

NOTES:

. . . .

DISTILLER: ....

AGE/EXPRESSION: ....

ORIGIN: .... PRICE: ....

SAMPLED: .... RATING: ☆☆☆☆☆

COLOR METER: FLAVOR WHEEL:

MAHOGANY	HEAT/ABV: _____ %
CARAMEL	
AMBER	
GOLD	
HONEY	
STRAW	
CLEAR	

FINISH
BALANCE
BODY   DARK FRUIT
ASTRIN-   CITRUS
GENT   FRUIT
05
04
03
02
01
SALTY   FLORAL
SWEET   SPICY
SMOKE   HERBAL/
                        GRASSY
PEAT   TOFFEE MALT/
                CEREAL

NOTES: ....
....
....
....
....
....

☞ **DISTILLER:** ....

AGE/EXPRESSION: ....

ORIGIN: ....   **PRICE:** ....

SAMPLED: ....   **RATING:** ☆ ☆ ☆ ☆ ☆

COLOR METER:

- MAHOGANY
- CARAMEL
- AMBER
- GOLD
- HONEY
- STRAW
- CLEAR

FLAVOR WHEEL:

HEAT/ABV: _____ %

BALANCE
FINISH
BODY
DARK FRUIT
ASTRIN-GENT
CITRUS FRUIT
SALTY
FLORAL
SWEET
SPICY
SMOKE
HERBAL/GRASSY
PEAT
TOFFEE
MALT/CEREAL

0.1 0.2 0.3 0.4 0.5

NOTES: ....
....
....
....
....
....

👉 DISTILLER: ....

AGE/EXPRESSION: ....

ORIGIN: .... PRICE: ....

SAMPLED: .... RATING: ☆☆☆☆☆

COLOR METER:

MAHOGANY

CARAMEL

AMBER

GOLD

HONEY

STRAW

CLEAR

FLAVOR WHEEL:

HEAT/ ABV: _____ %

BALANCE   FINISH

BODY   DARK FRUIT

ASTRIN-GENT   CITRUS FRUIT

SALTY   FLORAL

SWEET   SPICY

SMOKE   HERBAL/GRASSY

PEAT   TOFFEE   MALT/CEREAL

0.5
0.4
0.3
0.2
0.1

NOTES:

....

....

....

....

....

....

DISTILLER: ....

AGE/EXPRESSION: ....

ORIGIN: .... **PRICE:** ....

SAMPLED: .... **RATING:** ☆☆☆☆☆

COLOR METER:

- MAHOGANY
- CARAMEL
- AMBER
- GOLD
- HONEY
- STRAW
- CLEAR

FLAVOR WHEEL:

HEAT/ABV: _____ %

FINISH
BALANCE
BODY
DARK FRUIT
ASTRIN-GENT
CITRUS FRUIT
SALTY
FLORAL
SWEET
SPICY
SMOKE
HERBAL/GRASSY
PEAT
MALT/CEREAL
TOFFEE

0.1 0.2 0.3 0.4 0.5

NOTES:

....
....
....
....
....
....

DISTILLER: ....

AGE/EXPRESSION: ....

ORIGIN: .... **PRICE:** ....

SAMPLED: .... **RATING:** ☆☆☆☆☆

COLOR METER:

- MAHOGANY
- CARAMEL
- AMBER
- GOLD
- HONEY
- STRAW
- CLEAR

FLAVOR WHEEL:

HEAT/ABV: _____ %

BALANCE · FINISH · DARK FRUIT · CITRUS FRUIT · FLORAL · SPICY · HERBAL/GRASSY · MALT/CEREAL · TOFFEE · PEAT · SMOKE · SWEET · SALTY · ASTRINGENT · BODY

0.1 0.2 0.3 0.4 0.5

NOTES:

....
....
....
....
....
....

👉 **DISTILLER:** ....

AGE/EXPRESSION: ....

ORIGIN: .... **PRICE:** ....

SAMPLED: .... **RATING:** ☆☆☆☆☆

COLOR METER:

- MAHOGANY
- CARAMEL
- AMBER
- GOLD
- HONEY
- STRAW
- CLEAR

FLAVOR WHEEL:

HEAT/ABV : _____ %

BALANCE
FINISH
BODY
DARK FRUIT
ASTRIN-GENT
CITRUS FRUIT
SALTY
FLORAL
SWEET
SPICY
SMOKE
HERBAL/GRASSY
PEAT
TOFFEE
MALT/CEREAL

0.5
0.4
0.3
0.2
0.1

NOTES:

....
....
....
....
....
....

👉 **DISTILLER:** . . . .

AGE/EXPRESSION: . . . .

ORIGIN: . . . . **PRICE:** . . . .

SAMPLED: . . . . **RATING:** ☆ ☆ ☆ ☆ ☆

COLOR METER:

- MAHOGANY
- CARAMEL
- AMBER
- GOLD
- HONEY
- STRAW
- CLEAR

FLAVOR WHEEL:

HEAT/ ABV : _____ %

FINISH
BALANCE
BODY
ASTRIN-GENT
SALTY
SWEET
SMOKE
PEAT
TOFFEE
MALT/CEREAL
HERBAL/GRASSY
SPICY
FLORAL
CITRUS FRUIT
DARK FRUIT

0.5
0.4
0.3
0.2
0.1

NOTES: . . . .

DISTILLER: ....

AGE/EXPRESSION: ....

ORIGIN: .... PRICE: ....

SAMPLED: .... RATING: ☆☆☆☆☆

COLOR METER:

- MAHOGANY
- CARAMEL
- AMBER
- GOLD
- HONEY
- STRAW
- CLEAR

FLAVOR WHEEL:

HEAT/ .... %
ABV: _____

BALANCE FINISH
BODY DARK FRUIT
ASTRIN-GENT CITRUS FRUIT
SALTY FLORAL
SWEET SPICY
SMOKE HERBAL/GRASSY
PEAT TOFFEE MALT/CEREAL

0.5
0.4
0.3
0.2
0.1

NOTES:

....
....
....
....
....
....

DISTILLER: ....

AGE/EXPRESSION: ....

ORIGIN: .... PRICE: ....

SAMPLED: .... RATING: ☆☆☆☆☆

COLOR METER:

- MAHOGANY
- CARAMEL
- AMBER
- GOLD
- HONEY
- STRAW
- CLEAR

FLAVOR WHEEL:

HEAT/ABV: _____ %

BALANCE · FINISH · BODY · DARK FRUIT · ASTRINGENT · CITRUS FRUIT · SALTY · FLORAL · SWEET · SPICY · SMOKE · HERBAL/GRASSY · PEAT · TOFFEE · MALT/CEREAL

0.5 0.4 0.3 0.2 0.1

NOTES:

....
....
....
....
....
....

DISTILLER: ....

AGE/EXPRESSION: ....

ORIGIN: .... **PRICE:** ....

SAMPLED: .... **RATING:** ☆ ☆ ☆ ☆ ☆

COLOR METER:

- MAHOGANY
- CARAMEL
- AMBER
- GOLD
- HONEY
- STRAW
- CLEAR

FLAVOR WHEEL:

HEAT / ABV: _____ %

BALANCE · FINISH · DARK FRUIT · CITRUS FRUIT · FLORAL · SPICY · HERBAL/GRASSY · MALT/CEREAL · TOFFEE · PEAT · SMOKE · SWEET · SALTY · ASTRINGENT · BODY

0.1 0.2 0.3 0.4 0.5

NOTES:

....

....

....

....

....

....

👉 DISTILLER: . . . .

AGE/EXPRESSION: . . . .

ORIGIN: . . . . PRICE: . . . .

SAMPLED: . . . . RATING: ☆☆☆☆☆

COLOR METER:

- MAHOGANY
- CARAMEL
- AMBER
- GOLD
- HONEY
- STRAW
- CLEAR

FLAVOR WHEEL:

HEAT/ABV: _____ %

BALANCE · FINISH · DARK FRUIT · CITRUS FRUIT · FLORAL · SPICY · HERBAL/GRASSY · MALT/CEREAL · TOFFEE · PEAT · SMOKE · SWEET · SALTY · ASTRINGENT · BODY

0.1 0.2 0.3 0.4 0.5

NOTES: . . . .
. . . .
. . . .
. . . .
. . . .
. . . .

👉 **DISTILLER:** ....

AGE/EXPRESSION: ....

ORIGIN: .... **PRICE:** ....

SAMPLED: .... **RATING:** ☆☆☆☆☆

COLOR METER:

- MAHOGANY
- CARAMEL
- AMBER
- GOLD
- HONEY
- STRAW
- CLEAR

FLAVOR WHEEL:

HEAT/ _____ %
ABV: _____

BALANCE | FINISH
BODY | DARK FRUIT
ASTRIN-GENT | CITRUS FRUIT
SALTY | FLORAL
SWEET | SPICY
SMOKE | HERBAL/GRASSY
PEAT | TOFFEE | MALT/CEREAL

0.5 0.4 0.3 0.2 0.1

NOTES: ....
....
....
....
....
....

👉 **DISTILLER:** . . . .

AGE/EXPRESSION: . . . .

ORIGIN: . . . .   **PRICE:** . . . .

SAMPLED: . . . .   **RATING:** ☆☆☆☆☆

COLOR METER:

- MAHOGANY
- CARAMEL
- AMBER
- GOLD
- HONEY
- STRAW
- CLEAR

FLAVOR WHEEL:

HEAT/ABV: _____ %

FINISH
BALANCE
BODY
DARK FRUIT
ASTRIN-GENT
CITRUS FRUIT
SALTY
FLORAL
SWEET
SPICY
SMOKE
HERBAL/GRASSY
PEAT
TOFFEE
MALT/CEREAL

05
04
03
02
01

NOTES: . . . .
. . . .
. . . .
. . . .
. . . .
. . . .

DISTILLER: . . . .

AGE/EXPRESSION: . . . .

ORIGIN: . . . . **PRICE:** . . . .

SAMPLED: . . . . **RATING:** ☆ ☆ ☆ ☆ ☆

COLOR METER:

- MAHOGANY
- CARAMEL
- AMBER
- GOLD
- HONEY
- STRAW
- CLEAR

FLAVOR WHEEL:

HEAT / ABV : _____ %

BALANCE, BODY, FINISH, DARK FRUIT, CITRUS FRUIT, FLORAL, SPICY, HERBAL/GRASSY, MALT/CEREAL, TOFFEE, PEAT, SMOKE, SWEET, SALTY, ASTRIN-GENT

0.1 0.2 0.3 0.4 0.5

NOTES:

. . . .

. . . .

. . . .

. . . .

. . . .

. . . .

DISTILLER: ....

AGE/EXPRESSION: ....

ORIGIN: .... **PRICE:** ....

SAMPLED: .... **RATING:** ☆ ☆ ☆ ☆ ☆

COLOR METER:

- MAHOGANY
- CARAMEL
- AMBER
- GOLD
- HONEY
- STRAW
- CLEAR

FLAVOR WHEEL:

HEAT/ABV: _____ %

BALANCE FINISH DARK FRUIT
BODY
ASTRINGENT CITRUS FRUIT
SALTY FLORAL
SWEET SPICY
SMOKE HERBAL/GRASSY
PEAT TOFFEE MALT/CEREAL

0.5 0.4 0.3 0.2 0.1

NOTES:

....

....

....

....

....

....

DISTILLER: . . . .

AGE/EXPRESSION: . . . .

ORIGIN: . . . . **PRICE:** . . . .

SAMPLED: . . . . **RATING:** ☆☆☆☆☆

COLOR METER:

- MAHOGANY
- CARAMEL
- AMBER
- GOLD
- HONEY
- STRAW
- CLEAR

FLAVOR WHEEL:

HEAT/ABV: _____ %

BALANCE
FINISH
BODY
DARK FRUIT
ASTRIN-GENT
CITRUS FRUIT
SALTY
FLORAL
SWEET
SPICY
SMOKE
HERBAL/GRASSY
PEAT
TOFFEE
MALT/CEREAL

0.1 0.2 0.3 0.4 0.5

NOTES:

. . . .

. . . .

. . . .

. . . .

. . . .

Made in the USA
Lexington, KY
09 December 2017